Winning them Over:

Discover the Secret of Language That Changes Minds

By: Magnus Macarthy

various sources. Please consult a licensed professional before attempting any techniques outlined in this book.

By reading this document, the reader agrees that under no circumstances is the author responsible for any losses, direct or indirect, which are incurred as a result of the use of the information contained within this document, including, but not limited to, — errors, omissions, or inaccuracies.

Table of Contents

15

Introduction

Congratulations on purchasing *Winning Them Over: Discover the Secrets of Language That Changes Minds,* and thank you.

Have you ever found yourself bargaining with a car salesman or delivering a presentation in front of your peers or seniors? Have you ever wanted to negotiate a raise or made complaints? Have you ever argued with a close friend or felt that others seem to 'just know' how to deliver their argument convincingly? Perhaps your colleagues are getting promoted above you without any apparent reason?   Do they know something you don't? Is the answer simply because they can convey their messages better than you?

Believe it or not, you can get further in life by changing the minds of others for your benefit by learning and applying language skills that help to alter the minds of people around you. In this book, I will run through the techniques and strategies of rhetoric, a 2500-year-old technique, and how to apply them to everyday life. You will learn about the negative words you never knew you used and how to replace them with rhetoric to sell your products, yourself and succeed like never before.

Rhetoric isn't just for show; it's the art and study of speaking and writing well, being persuasive, and knowing how to present successfully. This technique aims to educate, inform, persuade, and motivate audiences and has been used to do so since the ancient Greeks.

Persuasive speaking is something you can use at any time in any situation. With years of experience in speech ghostwriting for prominent C.E.O.s, business professionals, and organisational leaders, I now want to help ordinary people, like you, to excel and succeed in life. Two thousand five hundred years ago, rhetoric was taught to everyone to help them deliver convincing and assertive arguments. However, over time, this skill has gradually become reserved exclusively for the rich and powerful. My aim in writing this book is to return this age-old skill right back to its roots, right back to the people, right back to you.

Before we start though, it's important to remember throughout this book that there are many things to consider when using rhetoric. To do so successfully, you will first have to:

- Analyse the situation that you're in – an effective speech adapts to the context of the problem.

- Determine the things that you want to communicate.

- Provide a strategic response with rhetorical tools.

As you analyse your situation, think about yourself. As the one speaking, your beliefs and characteristics directly influence what you're saying; gender, age, education, and experiences all play a part so recognise this from the outset. Your audience also plays an essential role in this 'game of words' as generally, the factors that affect you will also likely affect your audience, but I'll explain in more detail as you progress through this book. You'll begin to understand all the skills necessary to achieve success and the tools needed to convince people.

By the end of this book, you will have learned how to set up and frame a situation, which will allow you to use your newfound skill and consider the factors that may affect your ability to do so. For instance, location, events, political situation, time, etc. And how any or all of these factors may impact you and your audience.

You must understand the need to be completely clear of your purpose in addition to the necessary conviction to deliver effectively. Why are you saying what you're saying? Is it to educate, entertain, persuade, or instigate action? I'll show you all the elements required to give you a strong foundation in the art of persuasive speaking but ultimately it's up to you to practice and implement them.

Some people believe that rhetoric is at best a psychological trick or at worst, dishonesty or even manipulation. But when people criticise rhetoric, the irony is that they engage in it themselves by trying to convince others of their point of view; strengthening the argument that 'persuasive language' is a skill worth knowing; you quite literally can't argue that!.

Rhetoric is a powerful tool, and you'll learn how to use the tool for your self-promotion, selling products, and building the confidence to do so naturally and easily. As you make minor alterations in your language, you'll be surprised by the fantastic results you can produce. One significant and pleasant side effect of learning this type of language is that you'll become more confident as you speak. These are just some of the skills that I will endeavour to show you in this book.

19

With my expertise and guidance, you'll be in a position to equip yourself with the knowledge and skills required to convince others of all the things you believe in. Age doesn't factor here; it's crucial to start taking action right now, in this very moment. Remember, the longer you continue to use "non-convincing language" or (let's call it) 'bad language' to persist, the more challenging it'll be for you to bring about necessary change. So don't wait. Start a new, more convincing, more confident chapter of your life right now.

All the skills you'll discover in this book have stood the test of time and have proven time and time again to deliver excellent results for politicians, millionaires, C.E.O.s, and other highly successful people through the ages. Every chapter will provide you with devices to help improve how you present your arguments and convince others to believe that you're right. There's no going back once you start. So let's begin, let's win them over.

Chapter 1:

Rhetoric? What Are You Talking About?

Advertisers develop catchy slogans to get people to buy their products; Politicians deliver their rallying cries to inspire people to act; lawyers sway a jury with the presentation of their emotional arguments. All of these are modern-day examples of rhetoric – a language designed to persuade, motivate, or inform; this type of language, the language that changes minds, is "rhetoric." Rhetoric is the art of persuasion with thorough communication; it is a form of discourse that appeals to the emotions and logic intending to inform or motivate. The term *"rhetoric"* originates from the Greek term *"rhetorike,"* which means "oratory." Originally, rhetoric was exclusively used in public speaking. However, both speakers and writers use it extensively today to deliver motivational and inspirational messages.

Where Does Rhetoric Come From?

The study of rhetoric developed during the fifth century in Athens with the introduction of democracy. As the ancient Greeks started to run for office, they applied rhetoric to their speeches with the sole intention of winning votes. As the system of court developed, so did the need for persuasive speech. During the fourth century B.C., Aristotle, the Greek philosopher, wrote '*The Art of Rhetoric*'. In this book, he defined the concept of rhetoric as the "*power to discover all the available modes and means of persuasion.*" Aristotle's mentor, Plato, chose a more philosophical approach to rhetoric. Plato was sceptical of the practical, real-world application of rhetoric that his disciple sold, seeing it as a deceptive and superficial method of communication.

During the first century B.C., Roman philosopher and lawyer Cicero expanded on the definition of rhetoric. Cicero interpreted the concept as a form of dramatic performance. These Greek philosophers laid the foundation of the rhetorical tradition that is still in use today.

Why Is It Important Today?

Rhetoric is more critical today than you could ever imagine.

Even when you try to avoid those awkward arguments, those discussions at work, those ads on the TV, you get bombarded by rhetoric. From Politicians attempting to convince you of their ideas, marketers trying to sell you their products to friends trying to get you down to the club that you simply can't stand. In short, rhetoric can be found in all areas of life. Essentially, whenever anyone tries to persuade you of anything at any time, it's a basic form of rhetoric. For this reason, it's not only essential to get to know about rhetoric so that you can practice it but also so that you at least know how to identify and, if necessary, defend yourself against it.

Getting to know basic rhetoric can make you a better person

'Can it really, though?' I hear you ask. It's a big claim; however, there is an element of truth to it. The first rule of rhetoric is that you need to know your audience. If you're trying to convince someone of something, you need to be aware of all the things that could motivate them to change their mind. You need to appeal to their emotion, their reason. Can you convince them that you're an expert in your field, for example? The concept of rhetoric demands that you take complete interest in your audience and learn about their dreams, desires, and life philosophy. Take promotion as an example; I have mentored several students of rhetoric and told them to appeal to the motivations of the people interviewing them. I advised that they should research each interviewer and establish what work they were currently completing in their field and tie this into the presentation of their evidence, subtly and not so subtly referring to each of their motivations and portfolios as the interview unfolded. The results spoke for themselves when all receptive students passed their promotions the first time; those who disagreed and continued independently without further guidance lost favour with the interviewers and failed. On this basis, the results speak for themselves. I add the caveat that Rhetoric might not always help in a particular situation if executed incorrectly but it can certainly improve the quality of your life and subsequent opportunities presented as a direct result of the way you present yourself. Aristotle hypothesised that one of the most persuasive appeals of rhetoric is character or ethos. It indicates to the audience that you are of good nature and that you have their interests at heart. If getting to know people and having their best interests at heart doesn't make you a better person, then I don't know what does.

On the flip side, faking ethos isn't easy, and even those who advocate what appear to be bad ideas, generally have a good ethos as they have faith in their proposals. They project credibility and honesty even when their reasoning is faulty by nature. So, whilst rhetoric itself does not make you a better person, the desire to become better will make you a more successful rhetor. I'm sure we can think of a few tyrants who were good speakers.

You can be more powerful than you can imagine

If you have no desire to become a better person, this next point is undoubtedly for you. Rhetoric is compelling by nature, and having an idea about the ways to persuade can make a big difference between you ending up a cubicle in the basement or a corner office on the top floor, between an unscrupulous politician or a principled mayor in office. Some of the most outstanding leaders in business, politics, and arts were students of rhetoric. There is a word of caution presented by Cicero at this point however, '*Rhetoric with the absence of virtue can act as a time bomb*' – both in life and psychologically. Didn't Uncle Ben once famously say, '*With great power comes great responsibility*'? You may be able to

25

persuade your way to the top, and people have; however, you won't be able to fool yourself of the reality that you lack virtue, that realisation will eventually catch up with you, and your subconscious will destroy your efforts within that time. It's impossible to fool yourself, so avoid that reality check by educating yourself and becoming an authority in your own right.

As you continue to explore your new found interest in rhetoric, remember these points from this section.

Rhetoric and the Three Appeals

There are three 'appeals' when it comes to rhetoric.

Ethos – ethical appeal

Convince the audience that you possess good character and that you're credible so that your words are trustworthy. Establish this from the start or risk your audience losing faith in everything you say. Ethos is established before you present anything. For instance, you might be the C.E.O. of a company that you're representing. So, you're already a specialist in your area of expertise, and your ethos should be unmistakable. Some of the characteristics of ethos are:

- Appropriate familiarity with the audience

- Respect and trustworthiness

- Reputation and expertise

- Authority

There are specific ways in which you can improve ethos.

- Make sure that others are aware of your expertise by promoting yourself from the outset. For instance, make sure that people can access reviews, papers and testimonials about you if possible and appropriate.

- When you introduce yourself, draw attention to your ethos by smiling when you engage and ensure good eye contact.

- Tell personal anecdotes so that you can demonstrate to the audience that you follow your own advice. They're more likely to have faith your other points as a result.

- Ensure that all your stats, quotes, and facts are up-to-date and are from well-known sources. Choose reputable sources over social media for quotes, for example.

The source itself will have a credible ethos which, in turn, will enhance your own.

• Be unbiased by agreeing with several points from your oppositions argument. Doing this will highlight your crediblity as you'll demonstrate that you treat topics with fairness and consideration.

• Make sure you stick to the promises you make. For instance, during a session of Q&A, you might have made a promise to find an answer to a question. Make sure you do this to be considered trustworthy.

Pathos – emotional appeal

Pathos is to persuade by appealing to the emotions of the audience. Pathos has higher chances of your audience:

• Accepting your arguments

• Understanding your point of view

• Acting on your requests

You can improve pathos by using the following actions;

• Use metaphors and analogies when you speak. Linking your ideas to something your listeners feel strongly about can help to trigger the proper emotional re-sponses. A basic example of this could be, instead of using the phrase "They were ter-rible" use "They were poisonous." The au-dience is already aware that poison is in no way good, and it makes a flat sentence real, tangible and believable the human brain.

• Use words that are emotionally charged, like "The brush was a life-saver" instead of saying "The brush was amazing." The statement becomes more emotionally associable; using sensory and vivid words permits the audience to expe-rience the emotion thoroughly and subse-quently feel an affinity with you. The recol-lection of warm memories can also elicit certain emotions, and by using certain trigger words, you may be able to recreate those emotions to your advantage. An ex-ample could be, "......I recollect the scene and the smell my childhood home". You can very quickly enhance your message by building your audience association this way.

• Make sure that the emotion that you're trying to induce is appropriate for the context. For instance, positive emotions, like joy and happiness, need to be associated with your claims. Negative emotions, such as anger and hatred could be linked to your rivals suggestions, although this isn't completely necessary and I would recommend caution if choosing to do so as, you may lose your perceived good ethos.

* When you're able to, using images may be more effective than words at times as the brain process imaged up to sixty thousand times faster than words.

* What you're saying should match what you are communicating with your eyes, face, and body language, so bear this in mind during your delivery.

* Storytelling is a great way to develop an emotional connection, so you can build that trust by appealing to your audience's emotions using a compelling and relatable tale.

* You may also wish to target the audience's hopes by describing a future scenario when your proposed actions are followed. Search for 'make money online', for

example, and you will experience the full power of these sales funnels, constantly promising you ultimate death if you only 'click here'.

Logos – logical appeal

Logos is about appealing to logic (depending on your audience) and providing evidence to support your points. Logos assists in the development of ethos as the associated information will help you come across as credible and knowledgeable. Logical arguments are hard to argue with compared to passionate ones so the combination of both can be a potent mix. You can improve logos with the help of specific steps.

* **Be comprehensive:** Make sure all your arguments are straightforward and can be adequately understood.

   1. Use language that the audience can understand. Try to avoid technical terminology or jargon where possible.

   2. Use charts and figures; (the human brain processes images 60000 times faster than text.)

   3. Make the relationship between your conclusions and your evidence clear.

31

4. Use metaphors and analogies.

• **Be logical:** Ensure all your arguments make sense and that your evidence and claims are believable. Have a plan of how to deal with differing viewpoints that the listeners may have

1. Make sure that your audience feels involved by asking them enjoyable and engaging questions.

2. Talk about the opposing views; this should help to explain why your logical arguments are more reasonable and correct.

3. Build your arguments on the beliefs of the audience and views that are commonplace. For instance, the intrinsic value of a company could be that compassion is what makes them the perfect company. Use this commonplace value of the audience and liken it to a fact that applies to your situation. When encouraging your staff, for example, to join a committee, try to use their commonplace values instead of your beliefs. You could say something

like, "The committee requires kind-hearted and considerate individuals."

* **Be specific:** Base your claims on examples and facts. Your audience will accept your arguments more effectively in comparison to something non-concrete and non-specific. Keep in mind that the more easily evidence gets received, the more quickly they will accept your conclusions.

.

1. People generally cannot debate stats and facts, and they help to represent the truth.

2. Citing authorities on your topic will help increase your evidence's overall quality and, subsequently, all your claims.

3. Visual evidence, like videos and pictures, further supports your argument.

4. Tell stories of personal experiences or case studies. Audiences love to hear stories when you're a specialist, for instance, "When I went to Antarctica ...." In my experience, those with

authority to tell these stories are the most convincing and influential speakers. Google 'Andy Wyatt', an ex R.A.F. Red Arrows fighter pilot who at the time of writing delivers compelling talks about leadership using his experience to support his theories, therefore, providing a strong foundation of trust to his views.

There is some uncertainty around which pillar is the most important, according to Aristotle, logos was vital; however, it lacked impact and came across as too 'dry' when utilised by itself. So, make sure that you use all three appeals with equal measure, and you'll succeed in persuading your audience far more effectively.

The Best Approach to Modern Language That Changes Minds

As we already know that rhetoric describes language that persuades, informs, and motivates the audience. Examples of rhetoric can be found in countless places including, politics, literature, and advertising.

Rhetoric and literature

Throughout history, many writers have utilised rhetoric to capture the readers' attention whilst also communicating essential ideas of the subject at hand. Some examples of rhetoric in literature are:

- Jonathan Swift, the writer of A Modest Proposal, uses satire in the form of rhetoric. For example, Swift mocks the heartlessness of the Irish government by suggesting that people will start eating poor children because of the dire conditions of the time.

- In 'A Tale of Two Cities, Charles Dickens uses parallelism to stress the contradictory notions of society and continually uses the repetition of parallel sentence structures. The use of this structure, in turn, makes the reader deeply contemplate that period in time.

Rhetoric and politics

Rhetoric has been associated with political linguistics since the ancient Greeks regarded public participation in politics as an essential part of developing a civilised society. In the modern world, rhetoric is put to use by all political parties to enhance the chances of people voting for a particular candidate or for supporting specific issues. Some examples of political rhetoric could be:

- Rhetoric is regularly used in political speeches to evoke various kinds of emotional responses among the audience. One of the most famous examples would be the *"I have a dream speech"* of Martin Luther King. He said,

"Let us not wallow in the valley of despair, I say to you today, my friends. And so, even though we face the difficulties of today and tomorrow, I still have a dream. It is a dream deeply rooted in the American dream."

- Referring to the White House as the *"playground"* of the President would be a rhetorical tactic used by an individual who is in opposition to the presidential candidate. The phrase could persuade citizens to believe that the President is incompetent or is incapable of leading and utilises his power in the wrong way, and depicts the President as a child.

- The concept of patriotism is often used in political rhetoric to make other people less credible. For example, suppose an opposition candidate doesn't believe in a particular image or idea; The opposition leader could paint them as unpatriotic using words. The purpose of this is to dissuade potential supporters, and it often works, especially in countries where patriotism is strongest.

• U.S. Secretary of State William Seward tried to purchase Alaska from the Russians in 1865; however, the purchase was dubbed *"Seward's Folly"* by all those in opposition. The word *"Folly"* is negative and childish, suggesting a lack of knowledge with a condescending undertone. It was also playfully termed *'Sewards Icebox'* exploiting the low temperatures of the state and *'...the Polar Bear Garden'*, poking fun at the local wildlife. These people were utilising alliteration to support the stupidity of the idea. Incidentally, gold was found in Alaska soon after the Russians handed the territory over to the United States in 1898, supporting the prosperity of the U.S.A. ever since, not such a ridiculous idea after all Mr Seward.

Rhetoric in advertising

Rhetoric I can be found in product advertisements and various other types of promotions to convince people to buy items or services. Advertisements either appeal to consumer emotions or may even compare themselves with competitors to gain favour.

You may be slowly starting to realise that there is a dark side to rhetoric. While rhetorical devices serve a valuable purpose in making arguments effective, particularly in building your confidence and ability to speak well, they can sometimes be used tools of deception. Getting to know and understand these deceptive styles of rhetoric will help prevent you from becoming a victim of false or misleading messages. Unfortunately, advertisers appear to be the main offenders these days.

Some examples may be;

- An advert for a medicine claiming that more people choose their product over their competitor utilises rhetoric that doesn't demonstrate its worth or effectiveness. The rhetoric works however and, people will still be convinced to buy the product.

• An advert for children's food may say, for example, "Mothers who love their children buy X". This rhetoric persuades the parents who don't buy that product or brand that they don't care about their children enough compared to the other parents who do—a convincing tactic to win them over.

• A sales associate or advertiser for car insurance might use rhetoric to persuade buyers that they'd get less support for vehicle damage if they chose another insurance company. Whilst this may not be true, if the consumer didn't wish to check the facts, the sale would be more likely to occur.

The Five Canons Of Rhetoric

These are the tools used for the creation of persuasive speeches.

• **Invention:** This is the overall process of developing your argument, and to do this, you will decide upon effective content. Decide what you want to exclude and include. There is a requirement to balance what the audience needs to hear and what you want to say.

- **Arrangement:** After you have determined your content, organise your speech so that you can induce the most impact, thinking about how long each of the sections should be and the points you need to follow.

- **Style:** Decide how you want to present your chosen arguments, with some tactical thinking about how the audience might respond to your word choices and arrangement.

- **Memory:** Memorise your speech.

- **Delivery:** This includes projection, eye contact, gestures, pace, tone, and pronunciation. Ensure they all come together in a neat, practical, rhetorical package for your audience to consume.

Chapter 2:
Amazing, Awesome Alliteration

Alliteration is a technique in literature derived from the Latin word *'Littera'*, meaning "*letters of the alphabet*", created when two or more related words share the same first consonant sound, like *"fish fry."* It's the sound rather than the actual letter that's the essential element of alliteration. Not all adjacent words in alliteration share the first consonants. "Fish phobia" and "kitty cat" are good examples of alliteration, but not "thirsty typists" (as much as this might drum up mental images of sweaty workers slaving over typewriters!). It's all about the repetition of sounds. Some more examples of alliterations are:

- Allie loves all alliterations. (Alliteration where the sounds of "a" and "i" are repeated)

- She sells seashells by the seashore. (The repetition of "ee" and "s" sounds)

Why Use the Repetition of First Letters in Words?

Alliteration is a powerful and useful sound de-

41

vice that can be found in various types of literature but is mostly found in poetry. Advertises and businesses also use alliteration in order to draw attention to their brands and products. Several famous sayings and quotes use alliteration because the repetition of consonant sounds at the start of words creates musicality and rhythm. An alliterated phrase becomes fun to read, easy to memorise and playful to say out loud. There are certain sounds that can easily affect the mood of a poem and alliteration can be used to give a poem a smooth and calm feeling or a harsh and loud feeling. For instance, the phrase "Singing songs of the sea" uses the sound of "s." It provides the phrase a smooth and soft sound.

Alliteration is a noticeable and bold device, and could be used for calling attention to any subject. All great speech-makers use subtle alliteration so that they can emphasise some parts of the arguments.

Related Terms

There are two related terms, similar to alliteration. They are assonance and consonance.

Assonance

Similar to alliteration, assonance involves the repetition of some sounds. Alliteration consists of the repetition of consonant sounds at the start of the word. Assonance consists of repeating the vowel sounds within the terms. Poets use both assonance and alliteration for the creation of rhythm. However, the sounds found within words tend to make assonance subtle in comparison to alliteration. This is due to the sounds at the start of words being more noticeable and prominent. Let's have a look at an example.

Alice ate all the apples in the afternoon. (Alliteration)

We'll wait until May, when the shade helps to block the rays of the sun. (Assonance)

Alliteration is easy to recognise, which is not the case with assonance. The second example has both devices present. The repetition of "s" and "w" sounds right at the start of the words provides phrase alliteration. As both the devices are used here, the sentence has a sense of musicality and rhythm that it might not have otherwise.

Consonance

Like alliteration, consonance involves sound repetition. Unlike alliteration, it only uses consonants; anywhere within the words. Alliteration repeats both vowels and consonants at the start

43

of words. Let us have a look at an example of consonance.

All's well that ends well.

Here, the repetition of the "ll" sound occurs in the whole sentence as consonance.

The Power of Three

It's a fact that, as humans, we can hold only a certain amount of information in our short term or "active memory." A study found that the total number of items that we can easily recall in our short-term memory is three or four chunks. Despite such research, it's still common to see audiences being bombarded with vast amounts of information. So, now we know that your audience can only remember a small amount of information; there's no need to overwhelm them with hundreds of messages. The Power of Three is an underused, powerful technique that can be learned, practised, and applied to almost every speaking arena.

In simple terms, the Rule of Three is a general principle that states that all kinds of ideas presented in threes are more enjoyable, engaging, and more memorable for the audience. This is because the information that's presented in threes stays in your head better than any other type of information delivery. During ancient times, the Romans understood this and referred to it as "*omne trium perfectum.*" meaning "*everything that comes in threes is perfect.*" Today we're still aware of such sayings as "*third time is a charm*" and "*third time lucky,*" which also stresses the same principle. One can see the Rule of Three in every area of life. For instance, the three wise men, the good, the bad, and the ugly, or the father, the son, and the holy spirit, the list goes on.

What's the Effect of Doing This and How Does It Help Convince People?

There are two ways in which the Rule of Three will help persuade your audience.

Breaking up a speech

It's no debate that the best quality speeches have a beginning, middle, and end. The outline of a perfect speech comes in three sections – introduction, body, and conclusion. This repetition is powerful, and it can make any message more memorable, more persuasive and more entertaining (See how I've chosen to list three items here!). Furthermore, you should break down the body of a speech into three equal sections or three ideas that you'd like to present. Having fewer than three might not provide you with the punch required for the address, whereas having more than three messages also risks metaphorically putting the audience to sleep. So always use the Power of Three where you can.

Emphasising sentences, phrases, and words

When you utilise the Rule of Three for repeating sentences, phrases, and words, it enhances the critical messages of the speech. Why? The best explanation for this would be that human beings are great at recognising patterns. Because three is the optimum number of points necessary for creating a pattern, any information presented in three can form a pattern that people can remember more easily. As a result, all kinds of information offered in threes are far more memorable than those presented in groups of two, five, or four, for example.

The Rule of Three and examples

Some of the most famous speeches where you can see the application of the Rule of Three used to significant effect are;

Inaugural speech of Barack Obama:

'Homes have been lost, jobs shed, and businesses shuttered.'

Commencement speech of Steve Jobs at Stanford:

"It means to tell your kids everything that you thought you would have in the next ten years to tell them within a few months. It means to ensure everything is ready so that it gets easy for your family. It means to say all your goodbyes."

The Rule of Three will help you express concepts more thoroughly besides enhancing the memorability of your speech. So, without any shadow of a doubt, use it at your next address. The Rule of Three worked for Steve Jobs, it worked for Obama, and there's no reason it shouldn't work for you too.

Who Uses Alliteration Now?

Alliteration has gone through a great deal of evolution in our modern-day lives. All of us are introduced to the concept of alliteration through nursery rhymes along with other kinds of poetry.

- *'Three grey geese in a green field grazing'*

- *'Betty Botter bought some butter'*

Pop culture: alliterative name

A lot of thought and science is put into the names of consumer brands and products. So let's look at some of the brand and business names that possess evident mnemonic qualities.

- Krispy Kreme
- Dunkin Donuts
- LuluLemon
- Bed, Bath & Beyond
- Bath & Body Works
- PayPal
- Best Buy
- Coca Cola
- American Apparel
- American Airlines

There are also sports team franchise names that make the all-alliteration team:

- Buffalo Bills
- Los Angeles Lakers
- Seattle Seahawks
- Pittsburgh Pirates

We also come across alliteration in the names of film and music artists. Popular film, television, politics, and sports figures are provided with a natural edge on their overall popularity when alliterative phrases are used.

- Mickey Mantle
- Ronald Reagan
- Katie Couric
- Lucy Liu
- Jesse Jackson

Some of the celebrity artists who chose alliterative stage names are:

- Dr Dre
- Backstreet Boys
- Foo Fighters
- Beastie Boys
- Counting Crows
- Magnus Macarthy

There are several fictional characters in cartoons, movies, and books that have alliterative names. For example, the main character might have alliteration in their name, and who's more important than Spongebob Squarepants? Some other examples could be:

- Donald Duck
- Mickey Mouse and Minnie Mouse
- Big Bird
- Bugs Bunny
- Peppa Pig

J.K. Rowling, the author of Harry Potter, named the supporting characters artfully using several types of literary devices:

- Severus Snape
- Luna Lovegood
- Godric Gryffindor
- Salazar Slytherin
- Helga Hufflepuff

Alliteration examples in literature

In prose and poetry, alliteration and other sound devices, such as rhythm, helps in creating the mood or tone, emphasise specific phrases or words, and set the tempo.

Alliteration in poetry:

The following portion of Samuel Taylor Coleridge's *'The Rime of the Ancient Mariner'* demonstrates the poetic usage of literary devices based on sound.

"The fair breeze blew, the white foam flew,

The furrow followed free;

We were the first that ever burst

Into that silent sea."

William Shakespeare used "l", and "f" sounds to create images related to life and death in his prologue from Romeo and Juliet.

"From forth the fatal loins of these two foes;

A pair of star-cross'd lovers take their life."

Alliteration in prose:

In Harper Lee's *"To Kill a Mockingbird,"* the writer used alliterative descriptions of places and families to emphasise the importance of the entities in her novel. However, the emphasis was more on the "s" sound.

"...grass grew on the sidewalks, the courthouse sagged in the square... a black dog suffered on a summer's day...."-Harper Lee

Alliteration in speeches:

Because of its rhetorical nature, you can find alliteration in various famous speeches in which literary devices are based on sound. For instance, the Gettysburg Address of Abraham Lincoln causes attention with the repetition of "f" sounds.

"...Four score and seven years ago, our fathers brought forth on this continent a new nation...." -Abraham Lincoln.

Alliteration in content marketing

We now know that the primary purpose of content marketing is to develop a connection with the readers and inspire them to take action. We've learned that we can use power words, alliteration, sensory words, and various other writing tools and devices to create emotional and sensory connections with the readers and listeners. An emotional connection such as this is necessary for persuading the audience to take some action, from purchasing a product to clicking a link. For example, alliteration is a powerful tool in drawing attention to headlines, email subjects, and subheadings. However, alliteration can also help in emphasising a point.

"Smart speakers, as well as their speechwriters, sprinkle their speeches with carefully chosen power words..." – Jon Morrow.

How to Introduce It Into Everyday Language?

Alliteration is generally used to draw attention to the essential aspects of the phrase, but we've learned that you can also use it to create rhythm in a simple term. When using alliteration,

- Think of the subject that you want to emphasise.

- Think of the words that are related to the subject and start with a similar sound.

- Place all words close to one another in a complete sentence.

For instance, imagine that you're advertising a new clothing store.

Normal sentence:

I like this place. They have got a comprehensive collection of comfortable shirts along with some exciting and luxurious styles too.

You want to place stress on the fact that the store sells clothes that are unique and comfortable. To do that, start with "comfort" and find out other "c" sounds.

Clarissa's Closet has a collection of creative concepts and comfortable clothes.

In the sentence, the name of the store is catchy and memorable because of the alliteration. Try starting with the word luxurious and find other "l" sounds.

Lucy's Boutique has some lovely and luxurious clothes for ladies.

In this sentence, the focus is clearly on the "l" words.

Chapter 3:
Rhyme and Shine

Want to convince someone of something? Why not make up a rhyme? They may initially think of it as just fun; however, there is much more at play besides just sounding fun. You'll convince your audience more readily of your message in comparison when something is stated in plain language. Rhymes are easy to remember as they include their conclusion. For instance, "Red sky at morning, shepherd's warning" or "Birds of a feather, flock together". All provide a complete guide in the first portion of the phrase that easily allows us to remember the second half. It's been scientifically proven that rhymes do much more than jog our memory. They slip past the boundaries of the rational mind, and it's said that we are most likely to believe a message when someone presents it in the form of a rhyme.

This is termed the "Rhyme as Reason effect." It was proven to act as an effective persuasion technique when a team of researchers showed a group of volunteers ancient rhyming aphorisms. When they asked the group to judge between non-rhyming and rhyming sayings, they not only found that the rhyming ones were more trustworthy but are also more original, likeable, and suited to all the campaigns that they wanted to advertise. It appeared that human beings like things that rhymed. The archaic rhymes also had heightened positive responses from the group as they seemed familiar. All the sayings need to be entirely new for the listener to separate familiarity and believability.

Why Use Rhyming?

The rhyming effect creates a cognitive bias that makes people more likely to remember, repeat, and believe statements. For instance, most people perceive the aphorism "woes unite foes" as a more accurate one in comparison to "misfortunes unite foes" or "woes unite enemies." The rhyming phrase is also more memorable. Whilst these all mean the same thing, only one stands out. This cognitive bias is necessary to understand when used. It can help in crafting messages that are even more persuasive. Here are some more examples of where the rhyming sentence in a set of 3 conveys the message more powerfully than the other two:

- **Those who are poor in their condition are rich in their ambition.**

- Those who are poor by their circumstances are rich in their ambition.

- Those who are poor by their condition are rich in their desire.

- **Caution and measure can help you to win treasure.**

- Caution and measure can help you to win riches.

- Caution and restraint can help you to win treasure.

Additionally, as rhymes make messages more straightforward and more appealing to remember, various traditional aphorisms include rhymes.

- An apple a day keeps the doctor away.

- A friend in need is a friend indeed.

The use of rhyme has also been suggested to be an essential tool for education and helps students remember the subject matter.

What's the Effect of Doing This and How Does It Help Convince People?

There are various reasons why this effect influences most people.

It enhances the aesthetics of statements.

The primary cognitive mechanism that explains the reason why people experience the effect of rhyme-as-reason is called the Keats heuristic. The Keats heuristic is a subconscious mental shortcut that people use. They base all their judgments of whether a statement is true or not on the aesthetic qualities of the information. Individuals are more likely to use this heuristic in all situations where they lack the required evidence, motivation, or expertise to evaluate the statement's overall truthfulness. Depending on aesthetic cues provides them with a factor that can be used for evaluation. As this happens, the use of rhyme can make any statement more attractive, which, as a result, makes it psychologically more truthful.

The phenomenon was termed "Keats heuristic" with reference to a famous line from the poem of Keats, where he said, "beauty is truth, and the truth is beauty." It represents the connection between the related beauty of the language that is used in the statement.

It enhances the fluency of statements.

Another reason why rhyme can make statements seem more persuasive is the fluency heuristic. The fluency heuristic makes people assign more importance to the information that's easy to process. The easier someone finds a statement to process, the higher the chances of them believing it. Statements that are processed easily are also aesthetically more pleasing.

It enhances familiarity with the statement.

Another useful cognitive mechanism that explains why people perceive rhyming statements to be more truthful is familiarity. Generally, when people become more familiar with an idea because of continuous exposure, they find it more convincing. As such, when someone repeats a particular statement frequently containing an appealing and catchy rhyme, they'll find it more compelling over time. It is further supported by the fact that rhyme has been shown to help people remember essential information more effectively. It makes them more likely to repeat said statement and the rhyme in the long term by being easily recalled.

Where Can You Find These Techniques Now?

Taking full advantage of the rhyme-as-reason effect is relatively straightforward. Generally, if you want to convince someone of something or want to try to make your audience remember an idea, phrase that idea as a rhyme. It should be easy for them to remember and repeat. As you do this, you'll have to remember that combining rhyme with rhetoric techniques can help make it more effective than just using it by itself. One such technique is brevitas which involves the omission of all the expected portions of a sentence, like articles or adjectives, for achieving shortness and succinctness. Another technique is a meter, in which you will create a beat. Let's have a look at some of the examples of the

- East or west, our team is the best. (usage of meter/brevitas with rhyme)

- North or south, our team is best (use of meter/brevitas without any rhyme)

- Whether it is in the East or west, our team is the best. (no meter/brevitas but usage of rhyme)

60

- Whether it is in the north or south, our team is the best. (no meter/brevitas and rhyme)

Additionally, while taking advantage of rhyme, keep in mind that familiarity with a statement can make others more likely to believe and remember it. In simple terms, whenever it's reasonable and possible to do so, repeat rhyming words as much as you want to increase the likelihood that others will accept them. You'll also have to remember that as rhyming makes it easier for others to retain information, you could also use it in a mnemonic device to help you when you want to memorise or learn something more effectively.

For instance, if you are preparing for a test and struggle to remember vital information, you could phrase it so that it rhymes. For example, the mnemonic, "In the year 1942, Columbus sailed the ocean blue," helps you to remember the date when Columbus sailed for the Americas.

Rhyming used by others.

It's essential to be aware of the effect of rhyme-as-reason when others may try to convince you of something to make their message seem more appealing. Understand the original statement and do your best to mitigate the influence of this cognitive bias by simply being aware of the process. Do this so you can rationally assess the information. Merely being aware of the effect can help mitigate the influence that rhymes have on decision-making. Still, in some instances, you might wish to revert the information to its original form.

Change it in such a way so it doesn't include any rhyme; you may wish to use some more general techniques, like slowing down the statement to pick the message apart. In addition, there may be situations where you're required to 'de-bias reports for others simply by showing them that what they were bombarded with appears to be more persuasive than it is. You could use this technique, for instance, as you address your audience in a debate, the moment after the opposition uses rhyming statements for arguing for favour in their address.

In addition to deconstructing the rhyme, you can, of course, fight fire with fire. Phrase your messages in such a way that it also includes an appealing verse. Do this to win the approval of your audience using a similar kind of approach, which may (due to this training) turn out to be even more effective than de-biasing. Remember that if you choose this as your tactic, don't first de-bias the rhyming technique!

Who Uses It Now?

Rhyming is found in everyday life even without us being aware of it sometimes. Rhyming is used today to create profit and fun, so when should you use rhyme in personal or business persuasion? Firstly, similar to any other rhetorical tool, a little can go a long way. A subtle rhyme in a slogan or a phrase can help in making that phrase more believable. A rhyme comes with the power to emphasise a product or service or even answer common objections about the same subject. You don't want your overall pitch to be in verse; this will cause the audience to pay more attention to your delivery mechanics and wording instead of the actual message itself. Let's have a look at some ad slogans that use rhyme.

"I am what I am." – Reebok

"Beauty outside. Beast inside." – Apple Mac Pro

"Grace. Space. Pace." – Jaguar

These may not compare to Robert Frost; however, they're more fluent and memorable than other non-rhyming alternatives.

How to Introduce It Into Everyday Language?

It's not easy to introduce rhyme into everyday language as it's just too obvious, but cautious and subtle use can be effective. I advise you practice using it correctly before applying it to an actual situation off hand. If you use it without sufficient practice, the effect could be the reverse of what you hoped for, so be careful.

Chapter 4:
Analogies Are As Good as Gold

The primary purpose of rhetoric is for your audience to understand your argument and ultimately agree with it. Understanding only results in acceptance when the idea is well-targeted, well-composed, and where the conclusions are ultimately undeniable. Analogies are hard to beat in this regard, and their persuasive power comes directly from the audience reaching the intended understanding on their own. However, before getting started with analogies, we must first distinguish between their close cousins, simile, and metaphor.

A metaphor is a figure of speech that uses one thing to mean something else and compares the two. A simile differentiates two things to create a brand-new meaning while using words, such as "as" or "like." Analogies are similar to similes and metaphors as they demonstrate how two completely different things could be similar; however, it's slightly more complex than that. Instead of being a figure of speech, analogies are logical arguments. The overall structure of the statement results in a new understanding for the audience. As you deliver your analogy, you demonstrate how two things are similar or alike by stressing their shared characteristics.

The main goal here is to showcase that when two things are similar in specific ways, they are similar in other ways too.

Why Use Analogies?

Analogies help draw comparisons between objects or ideas that share similar characteristics or aspects; however, they are dissimilar in the other areas. Such a cognitive process transfers meaning or information from one subject – the source or analogue, to another – the target. This is done to infer meaning to prove arguments. In public speaking, an analogy can be used as a powerful tool to help speakers influence and guide the emotions and perceptions of the audience. Some examples of analogies are:

- An atom is like a mini solar system.

- You're acting like an idiot.

- The the athlete started sprinting like a bullet from a gun.

Analogies function on the assumption that if two items match, other attributes will also be the same. The concept of analogies is "A is like B." Saying "A is exactly like B" indicates that A is similar to B in every possible way. But as we're saying, "A is *like* B", this suggests that it's similar in only some ways. So, analogies are a comparison but are more appropriate for situations where direct correlations might not be suitable. The primary purpose of analogies is not only to show but also to explain. For this reason, they're more complex (and more effective in changing minds) than a metaphor or simile.

Analogies for speeches

Analogies are very popular in speeches and act as an excellent way of connecting with the audience to explain various types of complex concepts. However, not every analogy is made in this way. In the year 2010, a geometry teacher in Alabama was interrogated by the Secret Services. Why? Because, while teaching the students about angles, he used an analogy about shooting the President to explain the concept. So while analogies are powerful, they can get you into trouble if misused! Things to remember when using analogies;

- **Relevant analogies:** During your delivery, you may wish to use an analogy that ties to something within your current situation. For instance, you could choose to use an object in the room, the audience, or something that took place earlier in the event. The benefit of using this kind of analogy is that help's you to look more confident and present in the situation. In addition, it showcases your intelligence, you've not scripted these new words and you can adjust and take full advantage of your situation and surroundings.

- **Audience-related analogies:** This is thought to be the most powerful analogy technique for several reasons.

1. While most analogies need the audience to imagine what you're talking about, analogies related to the audience's life experiences are relatable and vivid. As a result, the audience immediately understand what you are talking about and make an emotional connection.

2. Doing this shows that you care for the audience and aren't delivering a pre-scripted speech; it's directly relevant to them.

If you know something about the audience, find a way to bring it into your speech in the form of analogy.

Example:

If, for example, your audience was a group of firefighters, you could use casual references for various aspects of the job. For instance, "As firefighters, you'll be aware that.... Etc etc.....' do your research on this one. This is a tie you can use for any purpose, decide upon the correct knot, and tie it well, or it could result in disaster, and you risk losing the audience's confidence.

You may be surprised to see how effective an analogy such as this can be.

• **An object in the room:** An analogy based on a particular object or thing in the room can be helpful as the audience can identify it more quickly than an abstract idea. Instead of trying to imagine the scene you want to describe, your audience can look at the object in the room and determine the value of your analogy immediately.

For example, I was once at a debate case to reform an agency failing to perform its job consistently. Statistics showed that the agency was unable to enforce the law 40% of the time. You can make various types of analogies based on this statistic; however, I chose to use an analogy that the debate judge could quickly identify.

"Throughout these debate rounds, you're using a pen to write down the arguments being made. Imagine that pen failing to work 60 per cent of the time. Surely, you would fix it or replace it? It's an obvious choice and is therefore obvious in the context of this agency." - Magnus Macarthy

An analogy such as this is tough to disagree with. However, it also makes the choice simple for the judge. Instead of thinking about the complexities of the agency, the judge can conclude, "I'd replace the pen, so why not the agency?"

• **Earlier events:** When something memorable or exciting happens in the speaking venue, you can use that for an analogy or comparison.

Example #1:

Suppose you are in a debate where the opponent team keeps claiming that you haven't provided examples to prove that your case is valid even though you offered examples in your first speech. In your final remarks, you could say:

"My opponent (name) is similar to Dory from 'Finding' Nemo. He's suffering from short-term memory loss. The main point of my opponent's argument is that I haven't provided an example, but I have done several times when I read a quote from an expert on this very topic."

Example #2:

When speaking directly after someone who has just finished their argument, you could use an exciting or funny point that was enjoyed by the audience to tie to your speech. This not only demonstrates that you were listening carefully to the argument but that you're able to read the audience, adapt to the situation and apply that same fact to your argument quickly and effectively, highlighting your intellect and superior ability.

This type of analogy requires a certain amount of mental agility, so either be sure you can do it before setting out or try to use it in a casual setting around friends and family first. Be careful not to offend anyone!

What's the Effect of Doing This and How Does It Help Convince People?

If you wish to make your communication more efficient and effective, the one tool you should master is analogy. Analogies are considered to be the water that surrounds the fish. You don't notice it, but it's essential for how you think and communicate. Analogies work because our brains are hardwired to learn from experiences and make judgments with as little thinking as possible. As you gain experience, you'll develop your own ideas of the things that worked for you and those that didn't.

When you encounter some new information, try to make sense of it by comparing it to something similar. We choose appropriate analogies from our huge internal database, generally unconsciously and instantly; this decides how we react to new information and allows our brains to accept what's in front of us more freely. There may be several familiar situations that apply; you, as the persuader, will choose the analogy for others to create that mental shortcut for them to take. To be an astute persuader, you select the best analogy, don't leave it up to the audience. There are five ways in which analogies affect the persuasiveness of an idea.

- Like any native guide in a new or strange land, they use the familiar to explain the unfamiliar. It's one of the most obvious functions played by an analogy. It's helpful to reduce the perceived risk of a new idea.

- Like magicians, who skilfully direct your attention away from their sleight of hand for maximum, magical effect, analogies highlight certain things and can hide others. They help in framing messages in a way that keeps them in the best possible light.

- Analogies help identify useful abstractions and make them concrete, making it easier for us to grasp the idea and remember it.

- Analogies tell a coherent story. Analogies are the distilled form of stories, and the majority of stories are only extended analogies.

- They resonate emotionally. All the feelings that are linked to the familiar get transferred to the new.

Analogies are subtle; they're like a spoon of sugar, making it easier to swallow complex messages. They provide help in bypassing the typical reaction that others may have against being directed what to do. Analogies are vivid; they help the audience remember all the key points you share as they use the information you gave to make their decisions.

Analogies are compelling, and once they've taken hold, they are challenging to eradicate. Indeed, all those who disagree might also disagree with your analogy. However, there is a 'first-move' advantage in this sense. When the analogy resonates, it is difficult to fight.

Where Can You Find These Techniques Now?

Analogies are found in various areas of life today. For example, imagine you have a client whom you have been presenting to for some time. You've used several graphs and statistics to sell your idea, but your client has become tired and somewhat disinterested in the subject matter. Instead of trying to share an excessive amount of data, information, and statistics, you could provide your client with an analogy for describing how the solutions provided by you could be used and what it means for them. Think of something that could apply to this situation to get your mind warmed up.

Analogies can help in persuading others, making it easier for people to make decisions. Unlike a simile or metaphor, they're like logical arguments. The persuasive power of analogy comes from the client reaching the intended understanding on their own. For example, before the technology of computers came into being, people used typewriters for the compilation of reports. Each time someone made an error, they had to either start again or use a white corrector for correcting the error. Think of the effort and time that went into typing a document. The typewriter is as efficient at choosing a toothbrush as it would be in place of a mop for cleaning the floors. In addition, analogies can resonate with others on an emotional level. Human brains are tuned in such a way in that we can recognise the matching patterns. So, the moment our brains witness a complex problem simplified with an analogy, it moves us emotionally.

Keep in mind that everything that we do, such as buying something or picking a partner, is based on emotion, and we back up all our decisions with logic. One of the reasons analogies resonate is because they reach both logic and feelings via pattern matching. Let's have a look at an example. You'll require effectiveness and efficiency for any new solution to have a return on your investment. Here, having one without the presence of the other won't work.. Trying to drive from Dallas to Austin within three hours is efficient. However, if you have a meeting in Houston as well, then you are not going to be effective. Efficiency is all about getting your work done in half the time. And, if you fail to use the saved time, you're not effective as a worker.

Analogies help to people to relate as they clarify and simplify the points you're trying to make. The analogy can help your clients, for example, relate to all those things that you are trying to present. They work so well that our brains are hardwired to learn from all kinds of experiences and make judgments with as much little thinking as possible. One more advantage of opting for analogies is that they are memorable and can be humorous as well. Picture someone cleaning the floor using a toothbrush, and you'll chuckle. People who are excellent in sales know precisely how to describe the solutions so that the clients can understand. When you use the correct analogy in the right way and at the right time, you can persuade others to reach a solution that will move them to saying "yes" to your ideas.

Who Uses Them Now?

Analogies are helpful in everyday speech, of course. But they're used in other prominent areas too, as I'm sure you've come to realise.

Analogies in writing and speech

Here are some analogies that make clear comparisons between two different things; you'll have heard most of them, I'm sure.

- *'..... finding a needle in a haystack.'* We know instantly that this isn't an easy task, and whatever situation it's been tied to is bound to take some time to complete.

- *'an emotional roller coaster ride'* - The ups and downs of a scenario or T.V. soap.

- *As useful as rearranging deck chairs on the Titanic:* You're doing something helpful, that in reality, makes no difference in the end.

- *'As useful as a chocolate teapot'* - Not very.

Analogy as part of the language

Making comparisons between two variable things needs flexible use of language. In addition, certain analogies are steeped in the culture of a specific time or place. All of this adds a layer of challenge and interest, especially when you learn something new. English becomes complex when using analogies as in everyday speech; however, you can become adept at enriching your expression and understanding with practice.

How to Introduce It Into Everyday Language?

Grammatically, analogies can either be spoken or written. Public speakers often choose analogies to strengthen their philosophical and political arguments even when the similarity is non-existent or weak. To build credibility and trust on stage, speakers link the main topic or idea to the audience's beliefs, values, and knowledge.

- Think about the demographics of the audience. What are their values, beliefs, and interests? Choose a suitable analogy

78

that the audience can connect with and relate to.

• Keep the analogies short and straightforward. Choosing extreme analogies may weaken your argument.

• Use analogies as a springboard instead of seeing them as the primary focus of your presentation.

• Use analogies from your personal experiences for the creation of credibility and authenticity.

• Play with them; they can be humorous and playful if you wish; they're yours.

Chapter 5:
A Sea of Metaphors

Metaphors are another powerful tool in the toolbox of rhetoric. They function as a lens to help others to think of concepts or ideas in brand-new ways. You can create metaphors using a combination of two disparate concepts or ideas. For example, think of the term "permission marketing." This is an interesting metaphor as it's easy to understand. The words used in this metaphor carry deep meaning by themselves. However, by combining them, the collective meaning is changed. Metaphors act as powerful tools of persuasion as they make people think about ideas and concepts in a completely different way. When you use the metaphor mentioned above, it gets your audience to question the traditional forms of marketing and consider how it engages people differently.

Simply put, a metaphor takes actions or objects and compares them to something familiar; but entirely unrelated. The comparisons used in metaphors are always non-literal, which makes them illogical. However, the meaning is still clear. For instance, Mother Teresa said, "*Love is a fruit in season at all times and in reach of every hand.*" Here, we know that love is clearly not an actual fruit, and the meaning of the comparison is well understood. Another example - "*..... is the black sheep of the family.*" As illogical as this saying is, we know the meaning immediately.

Why Use Metaphors?

Metaphors are figures of speech that are not true in a literal sense. They're not errors or lies either, as metaphors are never intended to be interpreted. Instead, they're figurative language intended for conveying a different meaning compared to the literal meaning of the used phrases or words. You can use them in creative writing, such as novels and poems, and other types of speeches, writing, and everyday conversation. Generally, metaphors are used to. Explain something or to illustrate It more simply by comparing it to some other thing. They perform various functions.

- They explain unfamiliar situations in meaningful ways

- They help people visualise foreign concepts.

81

- They create solid images and leave long-lasting impressions.

- They add interest and variety to otherwise dry conversation or writing.

- They are impactive on the audience and readers.

- They pair the intangible with the literal.

Figurative language

Figurative language is a technique that helps to supercharge the imagination of a reader or listener by taking a flat statement and filling it with colour, life, or humour. It's done to make the subject more interesting. It helps you to paint vivid pictures, hit the audience with the meaning, and become more persuasive as a speaker or writer. Metaphor is one speech device that uses figurative language. For instance, *"The first rays of the sunlight stroked my face gently."* Of course, we know that sunshine can't stroke someone's face literally (I hope). However, you also easily relate to the statement and imagine the sensation of the morning rays on your face. The use of figurative language makes a simple notion more vibrant in comparison to something such as, "I got woken up by the sun in my face." Although I quite like the simplicity of this statement!

This type of figurative language is called personification. It uses human qualities, like stroking, to illustrate some non-human thing or action, like the sunshine, in a more expressive way. It's a technique that's widely found in metaphors. Other figures of speech use figurative language, such as analogies, similes, hyperbole, and metonymy. All these are often mixed up with metaphors.

Difference between metaphors, analogies, hyperbole, and similes

Metaphor is different from the other figures of speech in a number of ways. Let's have a look at them.

Similes

A simile is the first cousin of metaphor. A metaphor states that something is something else, whereas a simile is used for the comparison of two variable things with the help of "as" or "like." An example of simile –

"Elderly ladies are leaning on their wooden canes listed towards me just like the tower of Pisa."

A simile compares two things directly using "as" or "like." But a metaphor states a comparison implicitly, without the intention of it being taken literally. An example –

"If he were a kettle, he'd be rattling; steam would be coming out of his ears. That's how mad he is ..."

Analogy

As we've already discussed, an analogy is like a turbo-powered simile. A simile is used to compare two different things, but an analogy is used to explain the similarities or connections between two things.

The primary difference between a metaphor and analogy is that while a metaphor uses a phrase or a word for the representation, an analogy uses comparisons or narrative for explaining the idea.

Hyperbole

Hyperbole is an exaggeration that's not intended to be taken literally. It is generally used more for humour, drama, or emphasis. An example of hyperbole –

"I was helpless and was quaking from head to foot. I could have hung my hat on my eyes!"

There's a vast grey area between metaphors and hyperbole which is often debated. But here's a fact for you – hyperbole will use exaggeration all the time, whereas metaphors use exaggeration only some of the time. When a metaphor is an exaggeration that's clearly understood, it's considered a hyperbolic metaphor. For instance, *"cry me a river,"* no one can shed that many tears so it's hyperbole. "your bag weighs a ton" is not a metaphor and is also hyperbole.

Where Can You Find These Techniques Now?

Metaphors are used in literature and speeches all the time, but to understand where these techniques are used, you have to first learn about the common types of metaphors.

Common metaphors

Known as direct metaphors or simple metaphors, these are the easiest to spot. They compare links and can be quickly established and easily understood. For instance, *"She was like a fish out of water at her new college."* You know almost instantly what this sentence means, even when it's not logical to compare a college student to a fish (in most cases). Some other examples could be *"cold feet," "night owl," heart of stone," "early bird," "eyes were fireflies," "couch potato," "heart of gold, and "heart of a lion",* etc., etc.

Implied metaphors

Implied metaphors force us to use our imagination. Implied metaphors don't make direct comparisons that are easily identifiable. Instead, they use implied comparison. A common metaphor is *"He was like a dog with a bone."* Here, the dog-like comparison is clear. On the other hand, *"He tucked his tail between his legs and ran away"* is an implied metaphor. The comparison with a dog is indicated; however, not stated outright.

Extended metaphors

Extended metaphors can be either implied or direct; however, they emphasise the comparison thanks to the extended length. Extended metaphors continue for several sentences, several paragraphs, or at times, even longer. Such metaphors are generally used in literature and poetry, where the writer wants to convey more commitment and passion to a particular concept. Here's an example of Emily Dickinson's *"Hope is the Thing with Feathers."*

"Hope is the thing with feathers

That perches in the soul

And sings the tune without the words

And never stops at all."

Dead metaphors

Dead metaphors are figures of speech that have been so overused or have been around for such a long time that they're no longer effective. Some phrases, such as *"melting pot," "it is raining cats and dogs,"* and *"you are the light of my life,"* have transformed from metaphors into dull phrases that you should avoid.

Mixed metaphors

These are when two or more inconsistent metaphors are mixed, often with humorous consequences. When used intentionally, a mixed metaphor might turn out to be a great technique of communication. However, when used in the wrong way, it could end up being a jumbled mess. For example,

"I can see the carrot at the end of the tunnel." – Stuart Pearce

Sensory metaphors

These metaphors use figurative language to appeal to your senses – sound, sight, taste, smell, or touch. They are evocative and familiar. For instance,

- His smile lit up the room.

- Her voice was silky smooth.

Who Uses It Now?

As we already know, metaphors are widely used today; let's look at some examples of metaphors used in the modern world.

Metaphor from content marketing

If you're a content marketer, you'll be constantly battling for attention. You have to make your words jump off the page and galvanise the readers into taking the actions you want. Choosing metaphors is a superb way of doing this. It's especially true if you weave the theme of a particular metaphor through your posts. It helps to give your writing a more creative tone. It can also help to make your messages memorable over and above your competition. Some good examples of this are:

"Want to bring all your ideas to life, to make them take up residence in the mind of the reader, lurking in the background, tugging, pulling, and cajoling their emotions until they feel and think

exactly as you want? Infuse them with power words" – Jon Morrow

"Smarter companies think of voice tone guidelines as the bumpers that you can find on a bowling lane: They will gently guide your communication in the correct direction and will also help content creators stay away from a gutter ball." – Ann Handley

.

These examples of metaphor easily paint vivid pictures that anyone can hear, see, or even taste. They also contain both similes and metaphors; however, neither included dead metaphors. Remember that good metaphors can also be powerful even when you tackle the mundane. Imagine how exciting metaphors are in the hands of literary fiction writers.

Metaphors from literature

Metaphors in literature have been present for centuries. They have helped develop glorious ideas and stories delivered directly to our imaginations. Metaphors make the words on a page come alive. So let's have a look at some of the great metaphor examples from literature.

"All the world's a stage / And all the men and women merely players / They have their exits

and their entrances / And one man in his time plays many parts / His act being seven ages" – As You Like It.

We all know these famous lines by the great William Shakespeare from his *"As You Like It."* Shakespeare is regarded as the king of metaphors and literary terms. Here are some from Romeo and Juliet.

"But soft! What light through yonder window breaks? / It is the East, and Juliet is the sun! / Arise, fair sun, and kill the envious moon."

The magnificent metaphors of Shakespeare have slowly made their way into everyday modern conversations. For instance,

- *"All that glitters is not gold."* – The Merchant of Venice

- *"Parting is such sweet sorrow."* – Romeo and Juliet

I could go on, but my point is that powerful metaphors will last the test of time and stay in the minds of your audience.

Metaphor from speeches

There are several famous metaphors from great speeches throughout history. Prominent leaders and politicians know very well that they have to capture the hearts and minds of the audience, and nothing does that better than a great metaphor. For instance,

- *"America has tossed its cap over the wall of space."* – John F. Kennedy in 1963

- *"I have a dream that one day even the state of Mississippi, a state sweltering with the heat of injustice, sweltering with the heat of oppression will be transformed into an oasis of freedom and justice."* – Martin Luther King in 1963

Metaphor from pop culture

Metaphors don't have to be intelligent and profound all the time. In T.V., movies, and songs, metaphors are often funny, sad, whimsical, and light. Writers of songs use metaphors to be more expressive, creative, and raw with the lyrics. Metaphors found in songs are meant to be felt. Here are some examples:

- *"Fire away, fire away*

  You shoot me down, but I won't fall,

I am titanium." – David Guetta

- *"Cause, baby, you're a firework*

  Come on, show 'em what you're worth,

  Make them go oh, oh.." – Katy Perry

How to Introduce It Into Everyday Language?

You can introduce metaphors in your daily language but you need to know how you should use them.

Metaphors in headlines

Headlines play an essential role in any post. If the headline fails to grab your readers' attention, the post is dead; try to use simple metaphors to make your headlines catchy. For example, I rather like;

- *Winning the War on Debt: Ways of being Frugal and Saving Money.*

Making an article or post metaphorically themed

This is a superb way of bringing a subject to life or for making a challenging idea more understandable. You can do this simply by first taking the topic and thinking of another concept that you can align with it. For example, say your subject is "writing a brief." This process involves a formula similar to cooking. So, you could use that as your second concept. Then brainstorm all the ideas and words that you can apply to the idea separately. The next step would be to look at the two lists and determine the views or comments that overlap.

- Diner and audience
- Recipes and set of instructions
- Ingredients and outline
- Result and outcome
- Secret spices and voice/style

'I've cooked up something special for you guys, now listen in...' a simple but effective way to pique interest.

Metaphors for making figures and facts come to life

Facts, figures, and data are essential for substantiating an argument but can be utterly boring. For example, if someone tells you that the earth's circumference is 24,901 miles, the chances are that you'll forget immediately; I have already. However, if you replace it with the statement – the earth's circumference is about 801,400 Olympic-sized swimming pools laid end to end, it creates a more relatable picture. Think of how we teach our children the concept of subtraction – "If you have three apples and I take one, how many do you have?" Nothing is different as adults; we need to visualise things. The human brain processes facts and figures far more effectively when someone anchors them with concrete and relatable imagery.

How to Be sure that the metaphors you use are relevant to the audience

Consider those you're addressing and the overall context of the subject at hand. For instance, if your message or post is directed at teenagers, you wouldn't necessarily choose a war analogy. On the contrary, writers who write about self-improvement often use metaphors related to battles. The audience strives to conquer their demons and decide upon new changes in their lives. It's better to use metaphors relevant to the time you belong to reflect the appropriate societal and cultural differences. Pay attention to the generational and age context of the audience; if your audience is young, don't choose old-fashioned or outdated metaphors that might leave them confused.

Using metaphors to make the dull sparkle

There'll always be times when you have to deal with something dull, and this is when metaphors become your best friend. Metaphors help you hold the audience's attention simply by shifting their focus from the boring to the imaginative. Compare art, religion, and science to tree branches, as Albert Einstein did.

'Einstein wrote: "_All religions, arts and sciences are branches of the same tree. All these aspirations are directed toward ennobling man's life, lifting it from the sphere of mere physical existence and leading the individual toward freedom._"

Metaphors can make your point powerful and easy to understand visually too. No one makes better metaphorical illustrations in blogging than Henneke Duistermaat in her drawn cartoon "Henrietta." Look it up. We may not be as talented as Henneke; however, we use entertaining imagery to represent our messages. But as you search for the perfect image, think of them metaphorically.

Staying away from cliches - don't over-do it.

There are certain things that you shouldn't do when using metaphors.

- **Don't overuse them:** Choose simple metaphors; if you add too many, your message will become messy.

- **Don't force them into writing:** Like using flowery words or adjectives in writing, it's better not to force metaphors as readers can see them a mile away.

- **Avoid dead metaphors:** Dead metaphors are cliched and have lost their ability to conjure new mental imagery. Most of them have 'kicked the bucket' or gone 'belly up'....

Metaphors and emotions

Metaphors can be used to express the feelings that someone is experiencing. For example:

- **I can smell the stench of failure:** Failure isn't fun but it doesn't smell (most if the time). So, when someone uses this metaphor, it indicates their disappointment.

- **Her words cut deep:** Words obviously don't cut but such a metaphor indicates that someone has said something very hurtful to someone else.

- **I feel blue:** As much as some of us yearn to actually be blue we can't turn blue in real life. Such a metaphor indicates that someone is sad.

Metaphors and behaviour

You can also use metaphors for describing behaviour. For example:

- Her **temper flared up:** When a person triggers your temper, flames don't spew out of your body unless you're my wife. You just feel angry.

- **He was fishing for compliments:** He's not trying to hook compliments out of the audience. This metaphor is a dead metaphor that signifies a desire for compliments.

Metaphors for heartbreak and love

Metaphors often occupy conversations regarding loss and love. For example:

- **She broke my heart:** No one can break your heart literally.

- **Love is fire:** Love is not fire in the true sense. However, a person trying to explain the concept of love as both dangerous and passionate could use such a metaphor. The fact that we express love using metaphors further enhances the point that metaphors support an emotional argument.

- **It's raining men:** Much to some women's disappointment, men do not fall from the sky.

Metaphors are present all around us. They sneak into our everyday lives in everyday language. They also help us to form impressions about situations and people. Metaphors act as one of the most potent literary devices and are vital in winning people over when used appropriately. The next time you want to grab your audience's attention to make them take action, quickly grasp the meaning of something or hang off your every word, use metaphors.

Chapter 6:

Similes Are Like Pillars - They Support the Argument

"She's as slippery as an eel." "Rob is as dead as a doornail." Comparisons are equally crucial in language, just as they are in writing. When it comes to comparisons, one of the most influential and most straightforward is a simile. A simile is nothing but a figure of speech and a type of metaphor that helps compare two things using words, such as "like" or "as." The main aim of a simile is to describe an item by comparing it to something unrelated. For instance, *"Life is like a box of chocolates"*, indicating how unpredictable life can be.

In the English language, a simile refers to a phrase that helps to describe something by establishing a comparison between two items from different categories. It's also used for exaggerating the quality of something. It's a metaphor that uses words, such as "like," "than," or "as," and verbs like "seems" or "appears" are used to establish resemblance and comparison. Let us have a look at some examples:

- She's as stunning as Angelina Jolie.

- Robby danced like Michael Jackson today.

You need to note that simile is present only when the objects of comparison belong to two different classes. When the things are from the same class, you can't consider them a simile. For example:

- Kashmir is like Switzerland.

- The pastry is like a small cake.

Why Use Similes?

Both metaphors and similes are used for comparison. The primary difference between the two is that similes use the words "as" or "like" to make the association. Authors use similes in various styles of writing usually with poetry. Similes are often used to help readers understand an object, character, or point of view by establishing a comparison between the subjects to something that the audience understands. Nevertheless, there are specific purposes why similes are used. Let's have a look at them.

Adds flavour to the writing

Making a poem more interesting is usually the main reason for using similes. Think of a poems as food – if there were no flavour or spice, the food would taste bland. So, you could say that the use of similes gives your "food" flavour.

Economy of expression

Writers describe feelings or subjects using only a few words and it's been found that similes help to give a more wholesome meaning using minimal words. For instance, if you say, "My body felt like molasses," the audience quickly concludes that you, as the speaker, felt sluggish or tired. The audience can also make other types of assumptions depending on what you say.

For comedy

You can use similes to add fun elements to your writing our speaking. For instance, "She was as useful as an unsharpened pencil, " implying that she isn't helpful at all. Such a simile can help add humour to your subject and grab the audience's interest.

Being on your toes

Similes, with metaphors, make the audience do some mental work. They encourage your audi-

MAGNUS MACARTHY

ence to utilise their imagination or interpret certain words in their way. As similes show instead of tell, they invite the audience to paint pictures in their mind. For instance, instead of saying, *"My love is beautiful,"* poet Robert Burns said, *"O my love is like a melody."* Here, the audience read the simile; however, they think about what the poet means. In such a case, different readers might come up with varying interpretations of their own.

No choice left

At times, writers need to use similes as there are no other ways to describe or express what they want. Or, what they want to say may have been already said over and over again. You'll have to be creative in finding new ways of conveying something that's already been said. Poets have lots of options as they use similes or metaphors in their writing making their process and easier one than yours..

What's the Effect of Doing This and How Does It Help Convince People?

Similes often use exaggeration or hyperbole purely for emphasis. For example, in this simile, "He *ran as fast as lightning*," the writer is not suggesting that the subject is actually as fast as lightning. However, the hyperbolic simile is used to make a comparison and craft a compelling description. Similes are a superb way of making any speech or writing more memorable and exciting without losing clarity. Most writers often utilise similes to introduce concrete images into their writing about abstract concepts. To understand its uses, let's delve deeper into the difference between similes and metaphors.

Difference between metaphor and simile

Figures of speech are phrases or words not used in the primary or actual sense. Instead, they're used to make a speech or writing more persuasive, engaging, rhetorical, and vivid. No poetry is ever complete without the use of figures of speech. In the English language, there are various figures of speech, however, the two most widely used ones are metaphor and simile. A simile is figurative language that puts connecting words into use.

A metaphor is a figure of speech where a phrase or a word represents an idea or object and determines the similarity between the two. In simple terms, a metaphor helps to illustrate meaning by creating images for the audience or

103

the reader. But a simile develops a picture while exemplifying it.

Basis	Metaphor	Simile
Meaning	It describes something or someone by referring to something or someone else which is similar in certain ways.	It is an expression that compares two different things, with the usage of "like" or "as."
Nature	Form of figurative language	Form of metaphor
Comparison	Implied	Direct
Connectives	No usage of connectives	Uses connectives

Similes are more evident when you compare them to metaphors as they It use of "as" or "like." These are the words that help you understand which comparison is a simile. Whether you're creating a story as an artistic exercise or trying to get your audience's attention, learning various ways of correctly using literary devices is essential. So, here are the key differences between the two.

- A simile is a symbolic statement where two different objects are compared with the use of words. A metaphor can be a phrase or a word that helps in pointing out the similarities.

- A simile is a type of metaphor but a form of non-literal language. But a metaphor is not a simile.

- A simile uses connectives, such as "like" and "as," which is not the case with metaphor.

- Similes are direct, whereas metaphor implies comparison between two things or objects.

Simile Examples:

- He laughs like a donkey.
- Trissa is as tall as bamboo.

- Thomas behaves as if he is the hero of the movie.

Metaphor Examples:

- My sister is Demon.
- Tony is a walking encyclopaedia.
- Thomas was the hero of the movie.

Simile: He's as kind as an angel.

Metaphor: He is an angel.

Simile: Love is like a war field.

Metaphor: Love is a war field.

Remembering the difference

Both simile and metaphor are used in speech and poetry. They are used to understand subjects by comparing objects, people, or actions; however, they're different. A simile is something that directly compares two different things. Metaphor is a term used as an alternative to highlight context or an idea to the audience. So in metaphor, the subject is considered to be something different; in simile, the subject is like something else.

Who Uses It Now?

Similes are widely used in speeches and literature.

Example of simile in literature

The use of simile is widespread in literature of all types mainly because similes help create vivid descriptions. Let's have a look at some famous examples of similes from literature.

- _"I wandered lonely as a cloud that floats on high o'er vales and hills."_ – **Daffodils by William Wordsworth (1807)**

- _"She entered with an ungainly struggle like some huge awkward chicken, torn, squawking, out of its coop."_ – **The Adventure of the Three Gables by Sir Arthur Conan Doyle (1926)**

- _"Time has not stood still. It has washed over me, washed me away, as if I'm nothing more than a woman of sand, left by a careless child too near the water."_ – **The Handmaid's Tale by Margaret Atwood (1985)**

There are numerous other examples of similes in literature, therefore you could say that literature is incomplete without similes.

Speeches using similes

Choosing the correct phrases or words in your presentations and speeches help to make a more significant impact and be memorable. Similes are figures of speech that can influence, inform, and inspire your audience. You can use similes in your business documents and marketing copy. We already know that a simile is a rhetorical expression used for comparison that differentiates two objects directly. Here are some of the examples of similes in speeches from history.

- *"Life is like riding a bicycle. To maintain your balance, you need to keep moving."* – **Albert Einstein.**

- *"Having a room without books is like a body with no soul"* – **Cicero.**

- *"Your mind is like a parachute. It will not work if it is not open."* – **Frank Zappa.**

Simile and metaphors are powerful tools. However, you need to be very careful when you use them. One of the drawbacks of using such expressions is that they take time, effort and creativity to develop. Therefore give yourself enough time to use your imagination, and you'll devise memorable speeches that will inspire, inform, and influence your audience.

How to Introduce It Into Everyday Language?

Similes are considered the easiest of all kinds of comparisons tools to use as they follow a straightforward formula – A is like B. A good simile is:

- **Clear and simple:** There's no need to start writing like Shakespeare, but think about all the things you are trying to compare and the context you're using. Do you believe the simile fits with the emotion of the scenario? Does it work with the individuals in the scenario?

- **Original:** It's tricky to do; however, avoid popular similes. Think of the imagery that you're trying to evoke for the audience or the reader. Try not to pick the very first comparison that comes to mind. After all, the first choice is always the easiest one, and it may not be as powerful as your second or third choice.

- **Visual:** The main intention of a simile is to paint a vivid picture for the audience or the reader regarding a specific situation or character. You need to ensure that the image is striking.

Similes are a beneficial literary device that can help spice up your speech or writing, but make sure you use them sparingly as they may become distracting.

Analysing a simile

There are specific steps that you can follow to identify and analyse similes in texts.

- You need to keep in your mind that a simile is a figurative comparison. Therefore, you want to ensure that all your examples use words like "like" or "as." Doing this will help ensure that you pick out a simile and not another literary device, like a metaphor.

- Techniques aren't worth anything if you can't use them to support your answer. So, it's always a better idea to ask yourself one thing – What theme does this simile relate to? Then, after correctly identifying what kind of theme the simile describes, ask how the simile represents the theme.

- You can describe how a simile develops using the T.E.E.L. structure.

T- The technique that is used

E – The example or the quote itself

E – The effect or your explanation, overall impact of the technique or the way the meaning is developed

L – The link or some explanation regarding how the example supports your argument

Chapter 7:
Amplification - True Amplification, Takes Time

Amplification is rhetoric that enriches and expands explanations, arguments, or descriptions. It's also known as *"rhetorical amplification"*. Amplification provides ceremonial amplitude, redundancy of information, and scope for memorable diction and syntax. In amplification, writers repeat something that's already been said while adding more information and detail to the description. The primary aim of amplification is to focus the attention of the reader or audience on an idea that they might otherwise miss. In simple terms, amplification is the process of making something more significant, more substantial, louder, and more critical. The use of amplification in literature indicates that the writer adds more information to a situation or sentence.

For instance, *"That dog is a great breed"* could benefit from the use of amplification. On the other hand, you could say, "That dog is a great breed, full of loyalty, intelligence, and health." Amplification is fundamental and is a member of the literary device tribe.

Why Use Amplification?

In literature, amplification extends a sentence to exaggerate, elaborate, and emphasise some points in a description, argument, or definition. Writers often choose amplification to help add more information to an otherwise average sentence using technical elaboration or embellishment methods. For a better understanding of the literary device, let's have a look at an easy example. Suppose you went to the doctor because you weren't feeling well. What would be your response be to the question, "What's your reason for coming today?" Your honest answer would be to say that you weren't feeling well. However, to make the doctor understand your condition better, you might add more detail. Thus, your answer could be something like:

"Doctor, I'm not feeling great today. My joints ache, I have a bad headache, and I think I have a sore throat too."

This amplification of your honest response helps in providing more information and elaborates on the basic sentence. Another example:

Actual sentence: *"The exam was very tough."*

113

Amplified sentence: *"The exam was so tough. The first part was challenging; however, I managed to answer some of the questions. But, unfortunately, I didn't have the time to answer the last few questions. So I have no idea about the answers."*

What's the Effect of Doing This and How Does It Help Convince People?

The primary purpose of amplification is to make a sentence longer with using elaboration so that the reader or audience can understand the message better. It also helps to make people understand what your problems are or convince your audience to do something.

Example #1

Suppose you're facing difficulties with a math assignment. You go to a maths tutoring centre to talk to the maths teacher.

Typical sentence: *"The assignment is really complex and demanding."*

In the sentence above, important information that the assignment is tough is presented. However, the teacher will need to know what made the assignment challenging to provide you with the help required.

Sentence with amplification: *"The assignment was complex as it included various complicated steps. I think I became lost on the third step; however, I'm not sure. I might have made some mistakes on the fourth step too. Can you help me to solve this?"*

With amplification, you can explain exactly what you were struggling with, and the teacher should be able to help you more effectively.

Example #2

Suppose you are giving a speech at a function, and someone from the audience asks, *"How did you get to where you are today?"*

Standard sentence: *"I have worked hard, and that is why I've attained this position."*

Once again, more information is necessary to make the audience understand your point, it's also not a very inspiring answer for a public speaker.

Sentence with amplification: *" I've worked hard to reach this position. I took and used the advice from my mentors and kept practising until I was successful, I failed on occasion, but now, I have attained this position and am privileged to give a speech here to you all today."*

Amplification can serve to specify with more detail and information.

Example #3

Imagine you're trying to describe how beautiful the day was.

Typical sentence: *"I was overwhelmed with how pleasant the day was."*

The sentence clearly expresses the intended feeling and sentiment; however, it lacks descriptive language.

Sentence with amplification: *"I was overwhelmed with how beautiful a spring day it was – the leaves were bright green, the soft smell of the flowers was in the air, and a cool, crisp breeze of air blew across my path. The sun was shining bright and shone beautifully through the clouds."*

A beautiful day can be projected off the page with amplification, making the readers or audience enjoy the experience with you.

Related Terms

There are specific related terms that you need to know.

Auxesis

Similar to amplification, Auxesis involves the collection of information. However, Auxesis is a particular type of amplification where you arrange words by importance, ending with the most triumphant or essential. Let us have a look at some of the examples of Auxesis.

- We scored one goal. And then another! After forty minutes, we were winning the game four-nil!

In this example, all the sentences are arranged in order of goals scored and excitement over winning the game.

- He was a little angry at first. After some time, his face became red. After an hour, he was burning with anger!

The sentence shows an angry individual gradually becoming worse in increments.

- We planned to have a regular coffee date. However, we then decided to have dinner. After a few hours, we were still talking, busy making plans for the next date.

This example showcases the development of a relationship as the date is extended and extended.

Imagine Auxesis as the commentator who during a game of football or horse racing becomes increasingly excited as the game/ race reaches a climax. They start slowly and steady and ultimately end up shouting really fast - this is what Auxesis is to me.

Congeries

This is another form of amplification where words are added to describe certain things in-depth. Let's have a look at some of the examples of congeries.

- She is a sweet, curly, petite, blonde, funny puppy.

- The speech was compelling, engaging, overwhelming, thought-provoking and, at times, very exciting.

- He was crazy, wild and just bizarre! One of the most amazing things I've seen! It was too much to handle!

As you can see in the examples mentioned, congeries add words and adjectives to enthusiastically describe something.

Where Can You Find These Techniques Now?

Amplification helps by providing more information for strengthening certain essential parts or points of a speech. It serves to exaggerate certain statements, which can easily underline serious or comedic intentions. It stresses the persuasive aspects of an argument simply by elaborating why they need to be considered. In creative writing, amplification can help to draw attention to the most vivid, compelling, or thought-provoking portions of a narrative. Generally, it highlights all those that are of prime importance.

Amplification in literature

Amplification is widely used in literature. It helps speakers illustrate moments and scenes more vividly and describe what is more important.

Example #1

For a simple example of amplification in literature, look at the first few lines of "The Scarlet Letter" by Nathaniel Hawthorne.

"It is a little remarkable, that—though disinclined to talk over much of myself and my affairs at the fireside and to my personal friends—an autobiographical impulse should twice in my life have taken possession of me, in addressing the public."

There is precise use of amplification in this passage. Instead of saying he's made up his mind to write an autobiography, the speaker decides to explain in depth.

Example #2

For the second example, have a look at Roald Dahl's "The Twits."

"If a person has ugly thoughts, it begins to show on the face. And when that person has ugly thoughts every day, every week, every year, the face gets uglier and uglier until you can hardly bear to look at it.

A person who has good thoughts cannot ever be ugly. You can have a wonky nose and a crooked mouth and a double chin and stick-out teeth, but if you have good thoughts, it will shine

out of your face like sunbeams, and you will al-
ways look lovely."

Here, Dahl utilises elaboration to correctly describe how an ugly person gets uglier and how a
beautiful person stays beautiful regardless of
physical imperfections. It is far more powerful
than just saying, "Ugly thoughts will make you
ugly; however, beautiful thoughts can make you
beautiful."

Amplification in pop culture

Amplification helps create exciting and compelling dialogue for lines in movies, songs, and
television shows. For example, have a look at the
speech of the critic Anton Ego in the film Rata-
touille.

"The world is unlinked to new talents and new
creations. The new will need friends. Last night,
I had an experience of something new. It was an
extraordinary meal from an unexpected source.
To say that both the maker and the meal have
challenged my preconceptions in fine cooking is
an understatement. They have truly rocked me
to the core. In the past, I have made no secret of
my disdain for Chef Gusteau's famous motto:
"Anyone can cook." But I realise, only now, do I
truly understand what he meant. Not everyone

can become a great artist, but a great artist can come from anywhere."

Here, the speaker uses amplification to explain how the world reacts when something new is introduced and how the brave critic needs to defend it. The speaker also elaborates on the tasty and unexpected food he had and how it altered his preconceptions. In simple terms, *"The meal challenged my preconceptions"* might have missed the more significant point – Ego realised that a true and great artist could come from anywhere. The audience knows that the speaker is talking about a rat chef and the depth of this explanation highlights how great and unique the little chef is.

How to Introduce It Into Everyday Language?

To use amplification, you need to:

* Determine the critical details of any statement or parts of the story.

* Elaborate on all those details or sections by amplifying them or just extending that point.

For instance, look at this story (sticking with the theme of rodents for a moment):

My dog was acting strangely. He kept moving around the refrigerator. I went to see what exactly was going on. As I made my way to the fridge, a tiny mouse appeared and ran across the floor behind the refrigerator. The dog went crazy and started chasing the mouse. After some time, he caught it and plopped it down on the floor.

In this example, the most cinematic and vital part of the story is when the dog chases and kills the mouse. So, therefore, you'll amplify that part of the scene.

My dog was acting strange. He kept moving around the refrigerator. I went to see what exactly was going on. As I made my way to the fridge, a tiny mouse appeared and ran across the floor behind the refrigerator. The mouse ran around the dining table, making its way between the chairs. After some time, my dog caught the mouse, holding it high in the air by the tail. He came towards me, sat down, and plopped his prize proudly in front of me.

Amplification pays attention to the most crucial part of a story. It develops a more dramatic and vivid image of what is taking place, intending to create excitement and entertainment for the audience or reader. For another example, have a look at the following persuasive statement.

"We need to go to the pool instead of the movies today as the weather is so lovely."

The most crucial detail of the statement is the persuasive argument – the weather is good, so it should be spent outside. To emphasise this, you need to use amplification.

"We should go to the pool instead of the movies today as the weather is so beautiful. There's a light breeze, the sun is shining bright, and no one knows whether it will be this good tomorrow or not."

As you elaborate on the persuasive point, it helps to amplify the strength of the argument.

When should you use amplification?

Amplification can be used in many situations. It is appropriate for further elaborating on points in scientific research, formal papers, and speeches. It's used for creative composition, like prose, poetry, plays, and dialogue to draw attention to the plot's essential parts. Amplification helps to describe a scene, character, or event vividly. It's also used in everyday conversation for the same reasons. It's unnecessary when the details don't matter. If you aim to be concise and straightfor-ward, avoid amplification.

Amplification can turn the sound up on what the audience needs to focus on and understand. It proves that less is not more, but more is more.

Chapter 8:
I've Told You a Million Times, Exaggerate the Hyperbole

Hyperbole is derived from the Greek word that means 'exaggeration', which is what it is. At times, you can quickly identify various hyperbolic claims by some trigger words, such as "best," "most," or "worst." However, not all hyperboles are that clear-cut. Someone might ask after hearing any hyperbolic statement whether or not it's true. In simple terms, it uses excessive exaggeration to make a point or to showcase emphasis. It's considered to be the exact opposite of understatement. Hyperbole is found in everyday speech and literature. It's a rhetorical and literary technique where a speaker or writer uses overstatement and exaggeration intentionally for effect and emphasis. When used in rhetoric, it's also termed "auxesis," which we have already discussed in the previous chapter.

Hyperbole is widely used in daily conversation to achieve a particular effect. But the interpretation of a hyperbolic example is not precisely accurate. It's an embellishment that highlights emotion. It's generally used to accentuate ideas, thoughts, and images presented in literature. The main aim of hyperbole is to add amazing effects to a text. It's of great significance in literature as it permits the writers to present something familiar more intensely. In simple terms, with the application of hyperbole, you can quickly turn a familiar feeling into something remarkable.

The use of hyperbole delivers a pleasant contrast as with this technique, things are explained by applying extra stress, whereas the other descriptions are kept regular and uninteresting. So, it quickly grabs the attention of the audience or readers and causes literary works to become more memorable for longer. Here are some examples.

- Richard was as heavy as an elephant.

- My grandmother is as old as the mountains.

- Decades have passed since I went to college.

- As I heard the conversation, I was dying inside.

- My backpack weighs a ton.

Bear in mind that hyperbole is entirely different from metaphor and simile. It doesn't make comparisons; instead, it adds humorous effect to speech and writing. It creates overstatement in addition to pointing out the characteristic of a person or an action. It's also combined with rhyme and alliteration at times.

Why Use Exaggeration?

While you might want to avoid generalisations in your speech, there are certain advantages to using hyperbole. You can use hyperbole as the descriptive language that helps create a more vivid picture for your audience and, in this sense, serves as a persuasion technique. Here are additional details that will help you on your journey

- It's essential to thoroughly learn the language that changes minds.

- As hyperbole helps express larger-than-life emotion, hyperbole is very common in poetry, novels, politics, advertising slogans, and politics.

- The exact opposite of hyperbole is litotes which indicates deliberate understatement. In rhetoric, elaboration is called Auxesis, whereas litotes goes by the name of meiosis.

- The primary key to hyperbole is not how a sentence is structured but whether, with the help of purposeful exaggeration, it can create solid impressions or feelings to emphasise a point.

What's the Effect of Doing This and How Does It Help Convince People?

Hyperbole can be utilised to a significant effect when you use it judiciously. However, there is a difference between misleading your reader or audience and using a hyperbolic figure of speech. It is effective when your audience understand that you're using hyperbole. As you use hyperbole, the intended effect is not to deceive your audience or reader, only to emphasise the magnitude of something with the help of exaggerated comparison.

Using hyperbole in writing

Hyperbole is an effective tool for all kinds of literary writers. It helps to elevate the prose and unlock more diverse phrases and descriptions.

- Think of an image or a character that you think maybe helped with the use of hyperbole.

- Ask yourself what elements of that character or an image you find the most important.

- Compile a list of illustrative comparisons.

- Decide which best complements the character or the image you want to describe.

- Use hyperbole naturally to fit with the flow of the more prominent statement.

With effective hyperbole, you can very quickly draw the readers' attention to the essential traits of the character or image that you want to highlight and emphasise their importance.

Using hyperbole in poetry

Most poets often get engaged in abstract thoughts and use hyperbole to make exaggerated comparisons. If you have an interest in writing poetry, try the following exercises to help add hyperbole to your writing.

Come up with a list of comparisons and images that you could weave into poetry to make the poem more powerful.

- Start by asking yourself what subject matter resonates with you and what kind of images it brings to mind.

- Now, make a list of the images of phrases that you think could be powerful and resonant in your poem.

- Choose the most effective and applicable examples of hyperbole to use in your poetry.

Using hyperbole in satire

Did you know that even satirists use hyperbole to demonstrate the extremity of an opinion or event they're trying to critique with humour? The most effective satire starts with a primary central premise that's based on a true story. It's then expanded to absurd lengths to draw attention to the essential elements of the story the writer is trying to make fun of. So as you approach any satirical piece, consider using these steps:

- Determine a central premise or a subject that you want to satirise.

- Make a list of all the elements you want to target that stands out to you as extreme.

- List all the hyperbolic comparisons that exaggerate all the traits you want to satirise.

- Choose the most effective and humorous to include in your piece.

Hyperbole is regarded as a critical component of satire. Coming up with compelling hyperbolic examples that can be included in your peace will likely be a brainstorming activity for you, so take time to compose.

Just like any stylistic choice, you'll be strategic. For example, you wouldn't want your speech to include only hyperbole, as the audience will quickly come to understand that your argument has no basis at all.

Exaggeration can make your subject more relatable to the audience or communicate your point in an engaging and vivid style.

Difference between hyperbole and simile

It might be hard to tell the difference between simile and hyperbole, but as we already know, a simile is a figure of speech that compares two completely different things to make something mundane more interesting. It uses the words "like" or "as", with which a writer can establish the comparison they want to make. For example:

- *She's as beautiful as a rose.*

Now, have a look at a sentence from a novel by Richard Brautigan.

"When Lee Mellon finished the apple, he smacked his lips like a pair of cymbals."

As you look at the sentence, it appears to be a simile:

- It has the word "like."

- It compares two unlikely things for enlivening the description of the author.

But the comparison the author uses exaggerates the lip-smacking noise by comparing it to crashing cymbals. No matter how bad Mellon might be at the table, it would never be possible for him to get to the volume of a pair of cymbals using his lips, try it next time you're with family. So, isn't this hyperbole? There is some debate regarding whether you can simultaneously use a figure of speech simile and hyperbole. With this example, you could make two arguments.

- The author's main goal was to vividly describe the sound of smacking lips by establishing a fanciful comparison between cymbals and lips. The fact that the established comparison amplifies the sound of hitting lips in an impossible way is secondary to the author's purpose, meaning you may think it a simile.

• The main goal of the author was to exaggerate the sound of smacking lips. However, the author does this as a comparison, which also includes the word "like." This could cause you to consider the sentence to be hyperbole.

Some experts of grammar might decide on only one definition – hyperbole or simile. But it is of more importance to determine the distinction between simile and hyperbole.

• Hyperbole pays attention to exaggeration to emphasise a point.

• Simile focuses on comparison for vivid descriptions and to cause the audience or reader to see something completely new.

Difference between overstatement and hyperbole

Overstatement and hyperbole are often used interchangeably. They serve as each other's synonyms. But hyperbole and overstatement have subtle differences in their use and intended effect. Overstatement is an exaggeration or a statement that includes an excess of what's reasonable whereas, hyperbole is also an exaggeration that's even more extreme. Hyperbole is a rhetorical or literary device, and both hyperbole and overstatement are figures of speech. Neither are meant to be taken literally.

Who Uses It Now?

Hyperbole is now widely used in literature, movies, advertising, and everyday speech.

Hyperboles in literature

Hyperbole functions as an effective literary device in several ways; As you exaggerate something, whether in the tone of writing, the traits of a character, idea, or theme, hyperbole can very easily capture readers' attention. It also makes the reader question the readability of the narrator, reflects on the writer's true intentions or provides some absurd humour for entertainment.

Example #1

Jonathan Swift's A Modest Proposal:

"I have been assured by a known American of my acquaintance in London that a well nursed healthy child, at a year old, is a delicious, wholesome, and nourishing food, whether roasted, stewed, boiled, or baked."

The satirical essay of Swift reflects his view of the oppressive attitudes and policies towards Ireland and the poor, blaming the British and overall aristocracy of the early eighteenth century. The quote is often regarded as one of the most famous hyperbolic passages in the literature. The author suggests using and selling Irish children as a source of food to relieve the economic plight of the people of Ireland. Indeed, this proposal is thankfully nothing more than a figure of speech and is an exaggeration rather than a literal solution. But the casual and practical tone used by the author is shocking for the readers, as is what he's suggesting and this, in turn, makes the passage even more memorable.

Example #2

William Shakespeare's Sonnet 147

"My love is as a fever, longing still

For that which longer nurseth the disease,

Feeding on that which doth preserve the ill,

Th' uncertain sickly appetite to please."

In this sonnet by Shakespeare, the poet uses hyperbole as a direct literary device for describing his desire and love for his beloved. The poet exaggerates his feelings to suggest that they make him mad and ill beyond help. But, of course, Shakespeare knew the readers wouldn't take what he was saying literally. So we can interpret the sentiment behind such hyperbole in two different ways.

Firstly, the readers can easily interpret the hyperbolic lovesickness as the method used by the poet to describe that his desire and infatuation robs him of logic and reason, and such a preoccupation and passion feels like a madness or a sickness that grows exponentially without a cure. Thus, the effect of hyperbole as a robust literary device would be pretty profound. Secondly, readers could interpret such hyperbolic lovesickness as ironic in the way people feel when impassioned or infatuated. In such a case, the poet could have chosen to satirise such romantic poetry with hyperbole, emphasising the significance of the final couplet.

Examples of hyperbole in everyday speech

Many people utilise hyperbole as a figure of speech for making something seem more significant than it truly is. Such distortion or exaggeration can help express strong emotions, emphasise a point, or even develop humour. Let's have a look at some of the examples of hyperbole in everyday speech. (There are many)

- The purse looks like it costs billion dollars.

- I am feeling so hungry I could eat a horse.

- I love you to the moon and back.

- The bag weighs a ton.

- I am going to die of thirst.

- I feel buried under a mountain of work.

- I feel so tired that I could sleep for a week.

- He loves her more than life itself.

- She's more attractive than the stars and moon.

- I have got millions of things to complete today.

- It was so cold that I could see polar bears with jackets and hats.

- She's got tons of money.

- His brain's the size of a pea

Examples of hyperbole in advertising

Various advertising slogans and campaigns use hyperbole as a unique way of attracting customers to the products. Here are some examples of hyperbole in advertising.

- *The best a man can get.* – Gillette

- *Breakfast of the champions.* – Wheaties

- *When there is no tomorrow.* – FedEx

- *The king of beers.* – Budweiser

- *Nothing runs like a Deere.* – John Deere

- *Red Bull gives you wings.* – Red Bull

- *Taste the rainbow.* – Skittles

139

- *Tastes so good; cats ask for it by name.* – Meow Mix

Examples of hyperbole in movie lines

Hyperbole can be very effective in the creation of movie lines that are dramatic and humorous. Doing so helps in making them memorable for the audience.

- *I'm the king of the world!* – Titanic

- *You sit on a throne of lies.* – Elf

- *To infinity and beyond!* – Toy Story

- *Love means never having to say you are sorry.* – Love Story

- *You'll shoot your eye out.* – A Christmas Story

- *What's this? A school for ants?* – Zoolander

Example of hyperbole in speeches

When hyperbole is used in a speech with proper care, it can help hit all your points hard. A small amount of exaggeration might be enough to perk up the ears of the audience.

- *"I think this is the most extraordinary collection of human talent that has ever been gathered at the White House —*

with the possible exception of when Thomas Jefferson dined alone." – President John F. Kennedy.

• *"Please sit down because having produced nine million award shows; I know the producer's up there saying, 'Hurry, say thanks fast."* – Dick Clark.

Example of hyperbole in songs

Like a well-delivered speech, hyperbole can also help to paint vivid pictures or express strong emotions in the song lyrics.

• *"But I would walk 500 miles/ And I would walk 500 more/ Just to be the man who walks a thousand miles/ to fall down at your door."* – I am Gonna Be by The Proclaimers.

• *"I would fly to the moon and back/ if you'll be If you'll be my baby/ Got a ticket for a world where/ we belong/ So would you be my baby"* – To the Moon and Back by Savage Garden.

How to Introduce It Into Everyday Language?

Hyperbole is over the top and is never meant to be taken literally. You need to keep your ears open to determine the exaggeration in different sources, from plays and poetry to everyday commercials. You can use hyperbole to show contrast or inject humour and feeling into what you say or write. When you use it ideally, the effect of embellishment can be empathic and purposeful, making the audience or reader pay attention. However, make sure you don't overdo it. People and writers, in general, exaggerate accounts of their experiences for communication. Hyperbole can provide them with an opportunity to compensate for the fact that you cannot reproduce authentic experiences in written or spoken language satisfactorily. Ensure that the elaboration you choose matches the context of what you want to say.

Chapter 9:
Happy Personification

"You can never deny laughter. When it comes, it will plop down in your favourite chair and will stay as long as it wants to." – Stephen King.

So, you've been asked to persuade a friend that there's no better medicine than laughter. You try to use several facts to get your point across. What do you think would happen if you thought of laughter as a human being, just like the example mentioned above? Do you think it would help you in connecting with your audience or readers? That's what personification is all about. It can do wonders if you use it well. Whether you use it in a persuasive essay or speech, personification can help convey the overall message in a very effective way.

Personification is an imperative figure of speech, and with the application of this literary tool, animals, ideas, and objects obtain human qualities. In simple terms, views, along with the objects, get personified. As a result, the readers establish a connection with all the things you describe. The use of personification in literature has a significant impact as it can showcase an entity, non-human in nature, more vividly with human attributes. The primary aim of this literary device is to grab the reader's attention and make the description more remarkable and prominent. In short, it helps boost the sensitivity and emotion of the reader. Some examples of personification are:

- *The cold wind whispered in her ears.*

- *Time and tide wait for none.*

- *The cat danced with enthusiasm.*

- *The fire swallowed the entire house.*

In the examples mentioned above, the objects, tide, time, and wind, are expressed to easily connect and relate to the reader's emotion. Although personification is often a decorative device, it adds more profound meaning to the overall speech or writing. It causes the readers to remember the text for longer. Poets and writers prefer adding this device in their works as it helps to describe inanimate things as living entities. It's also used to make actions and nature clearer. Any reader can understand the traits of human beings. So, non-living entities are treated as human beings, which is why the technique is termed personification.

The use of personification in literature is rife. Henry Wadsworth Longfellow's poem "Paul Revere's Ride" is an excellent example of personification.

"And the meeting-house windows, blank and bare,

Gaze at him with a spectral glare

As if they already stood aghast

At the bloody work, they would look upon."

In this poem, the windows are personified and help in making the writing feel more natural. Another famous poem by Emily Dickinson named *"There's a Certain Slant of Light"* is an excellent example of personification.

"When it comes, the landscape listens,

Shadows hold their breath."

In this, the shadows and landscape get the qualities of humans and make the lines more alive.

Why Use Personification?

One of the simplest ways of thinking about personification is to consider the characters of some of our favourite childhood cartoons: Mickey and Minnie Mouse, Donald Duck, or Teenage Mutant Ninja Turtles. As a form of hyperbole, we all know that these animals can't go on madcap adventures to Disney World, speak English, or use martial arts to fight crime. However, their personification makes them feel more human to us. Besides being an artful form of speaking, you can utilise personification to make your point. It's no surprise that your audience easily understand a complex idea when providing it with human characteristics and qualities. The primary purpose of persuasive writing mainly includes:

- Getting the reader in your shoes

- Convincing the readers to see your point of view

- Keeping the readers or audience interested in what you write or say

- Making the audience or readers believe in your ideas

- Understanding both sides of the argument

- Getting the attention of a new audience

Personification is regularly used in persuasive writing. But, as we all know, it's also a figure of speech; it has the power to help create unique descriptions that allow the audience or readers to connect to what you have to say quickly. It's thought to be one of the most powerful ways of conveying your messages to the audience.

Adds life to non-living things

Personification adds life to non-living things or places when used in persuasive writing or speaking and hugely increases your chances of relating to the audience. It persuades them to understand your views by creating a vivid, relatable image in their minds. Personification causes people to think about the things you want to say and prove. For example, if you're going to persuade a friend to drink tea, you need to convey the importance of the suggestion. However, the moment you try to personify tea and then convince your friend, they'll quickly understand your viewpoint. '*A cup of tea is a hug in a mug*'. Personifying tea as a powerful stress reliever through a hug will at least force your friend to consider having some tea, and at best, make them actually have some tea at some point.

You could say that personification helps in pulling at your heartstrings. All of us understand

147

something when presented with live examples about precisely how this technique functions. It adds life to objects and enhances the quality of your content.

Relevance of personification in persuasive writing

As we now have some clarity around personification and persuasive writing, let's look at its importance. Here are some points that highlight the importance of personification in persuasive writing.

- **Robust and powerful:** Personification adds power to writing to convince the readers.

- **Relatable:** Personification plays an essential role in making your subject matter relatable and helps in building strong emotional connections. It's critical to have the readers on the same page at the end.

(Metaphorically speaking!)

- **Creating better perceptions:** As you add human characteristics and traits to an object, people understand them better. Therefore, it creates better perceptions than those attached to non-living things.

- **Creates a better impression:** Personification helps to stir the emotions of the reader. It also helps to make a long-lasting impact on their thoughts. The technique works well to persuade the readers in whatever you choose to convince them of.

What's the Effect of Doing This and How Does It Help Convince People?

Personification helps give a voice to all those things that don't have one of their own. For example, we know smoking is bad for our health. Everyone's aware of this, but smokers don't care. If you personify smoking, it helps evoke a vivid image of the consequences of smoking in your mind's eye. As a result, it becomes easier to persuade your readers of this fact. Persuasive writing comes in various forms, essays, speeches, or poems. Regardless of the type of writing, personification is helpful all the time.

Direction of influence

Persuasive speaking and writing aims to influence your target audience to think in a certain way. Persuasion should always evoke precise emotions in the reader's mind, and it makes the task of stimulating emotions easier. It can help

149

the readers to see everything you want them to see. Let's have a look at an example with a tinge of personification.

"Nature is the epitome of calmness and beauty; she provides us with food to satiate our hunger and blesses us with shade to protect us from the summer heat. She provides us with everything that we need to sustain on earth. Yet, she screams in extreme pain as we cut down trees or just burn her down to make more room for the new buildings. She is no damsel in distress. She is the fearless queen who will surely take her revenge when the perfect time comes. Human beings cannot live without her. However, she can live without us as she is the creator and the destroyer of this planet. We all are eternally grateful and dependent on her."

The example above personifies the world as a fiery, strong woman who feeds and protects us. The readers understand the point better as they feel connected to all the things you convey. You're not only saying something, you're presenting a whole new picture to the readers.

Creation of fiction using facts

Say if your persuasive writing topic was related to animal cruelty, personification is one of the best weapons you can use for nailing your content. You allow the readers to imagine the animal as a human being. Of course, animal nature is very different from humans', but it becomes easier to create a bond between man and the animal as you personify them. This technique might seem fictitious; however, it can strike an emotional chord in the audience and help the readers look at things from an abstract point of view and helps explain how certain things exist as a whole.

Personification blurs reality and stretches the imagination. For example, you could take an inanimate object and describe it as if all its reactions and actions were human-like.

Incorporation of appeal

The persuasive writing you present to your readers is unsuitable if it fails to appeal to the target audience. Never expect to persuade the readers of a topic if it's boring. Personification makes an inanimate object into something with soul and spirit. When there's an absence of personification, the writing may seem bland to read. Human nature is something that all of us are aware of, have a vested interest in or should do. It reflects confidence in what you're saying and hooks the audience to the main content.

"The wall, being formidable as ever, mocked our efforts to navigate the less-travelled roads."

This is an excellent example of personification that is witty. The wall does not appear or mock out of the blue. However, *"We came to a dead end."* doesn't quite hit the mark somehow. Instead, it creates a visual connection by attaching human traits to an inanimate object. Some other common examples of personification that can be used in persuasive delivery:

- *The cat danced better than a professional dancer.*

- *The waves were dancing to the tune of the breeze.*

If you want to add deeper meaning to your persuasive writing, use personification without giving it a second thought. For example, you can personify objects like wind, time, and rain to stir up the readers' emotions. It helps create a long-lasting impression in the readers' minds and helps persuade them without additional effort.

Where Can You Find These Techniques Now?

You can find personification everywhere. The literary tool helps to add fun and interest to stories, poems, advertising, and everyday language.

Example of personification in books and poetry

There are several examples of personification when it comes to literature.

Example #1

"The fog comes

On little cat feet.

It sits looking

over harbor and city

on silent haunches

and then moves on."

This example is from Carl Sandburg's poem "The Fog." Here, fog is provided with human-like abilities to sit and look.

Example #2

"Hey, diddle, diddle,

The cat and the fiddle,

The cow jumped over the moon;

The little dog laughed

To see such sport,

And the dish ran away with the spoon."

The example mentioned above is from the famous nursery rhyme "*Hey Diddle Diddle.*" In this, both objects and animals can do things that human beings do.

Example of personification in advertising.

You can also find personification in advertising. Let's have a look at some of the examples.

- *Milk's favourite cookie* – Oreo

- *The car that cares* – Kia

- *Nothing hugs like Huggies* – Huggies diapers

- *Kleenex says bless you* – Kleenex facial tissues

- *It's what happy tastes like* – Carvel ice cream

- *Gatorade always wins* – Gatorade

How to Introduce It Into Everyday Language?

There are two ways you can approach personification. Firstly by speaking in the third person and personifying an inanimate object, abstract thought, or animal. In this case, as you speak as someone or something else, the audience will project their reactions on what you are trying to be and not onto you as the speaker. It's a helpful technique to deflect negative responses. In addition, as you speak like someone else, the audience is less likely to blame you for the words used. Secondly, you could approach assigning human-like qualities to an idea or an object, deflecting negativity while adding to the strength of your views and comments. Here are some more examples of personification that you can find in our everyday lives.

- *The wind howled in the night.*

- *The door protested as it opened.*

- *My house is my friend who protects me.*

- *The staircase groaned as we walked down them.*

Chapter 10:
Parallel Structure, Powerful Results

Parallelism is nothing but the repetition of grammatical elements in speaking and writing. It influences the grammatical structure of the sentences; however, it also impacts on the meaning of the ideas and thoughts being presented. When someone uses parallelism as a figure of speech, it extends beyond just a sentence structure technique. For example, you might repeat phrases or words to add emphasis or use it to create a parallel position between opposing ideas with grammatical elements as a way of emphasising the point. It takes various forms in literature; antithesis, anaphora, epistrophe, and asyndeton.

All these figures of speech and literary devices are specific types of parallelism. Possibly the most famous example related to parallelism is the statement from Neil Armstrong as he stepped onto the moon – *"It's one small step for man, one giant leap for mankind."* The sentence's structure of   two phrases is the same because of the repeated use of the word "one." This engages the audience's attention and emphasises the contrast between "*giant leap for mankind*" and "*small step for man.*" The significance of the entire event and the meaning of the statement is enhanced with parallelism.

Why Use Parallelism?

Parallelism uses similar phrases, words, or clauses to show that your ideas have the same level of importance. Such a structure helps to enhance readability by providing a natural flow to your work. For native English speakers, parallelism is instinctive. They say, "I like writing, reading, and painting" in place of "I like to write, read, and paint."

Difference between repetition and parallelism

It's tough to differentiate between repetition and parallelism. They're similar in that both functions are based on something repeated for effect. Repetition features the intentional use of a phrase or word, two or more times in very close proximity, whilst parallelism includes the repetition of phrases or words, it also needs to reflect the repetition of structural or grammatical elements.

A great way to determine the difference between repetition and parallelism is demonstrated in a monologue spoken by the title character in William Shakespeare's Macbeth. The famous line, "*Tomorrow, and tomorrow, and tomorrow*" shows the repetition of words and features parallelism as the grammatical structure of phrasing, using "*and*" in conjunction. Such grammatical similarities help enhance the rhythm of the phrase and emphasise the meaning and concept of *"tomorrow"* as a repeating, ongoing aggregate of experience and time.

Another line from Macbeth's soliloquy shows repetition and no parallelism – "*Out, out, brief candle!*" In this line, "*out*" has been repeated twice; however, there's no sign of a repeating grammatical component. Although the effect of this repetition is to stress the word "*out*" about extinguishing the candle, indicating death, there is much less poetic nature in the line than the parallelism and repetition of the phrase "*tomorrow.*" So, as literary devices, repetition emphasises a phrase or word and can also reinforce the meaning. But parallelism helps to add deeper meaning with the repetiton of grammatical structure.

What's the Effect of Doing This and How Does It Help Convince People?

Parallelism is essential as it can make a piece of writing much easier to understand. It allows your audience to understand what's occurring, what's taking place, and who the subject is.

Creation of a sense of rhythm

Writers can create a sense of rhythm in their work with parallelism. Repetition of grammatical elements, such as sounds, words, verb, or noun phrases, helps add pace to the writing. It adds to language's poetic or artistic value while permitting the writer to elaborate or reinforce a particular idea.

Creation of a sense of relationship

Parallelism permits writers to develop a relationship between phrases, words, and sentences, which helps establish relationships between ideas and things. You can do it with contrast or comparison, either within one sentence or a group of sentences. With repetition of grammatical elements, writers draw the readers' attention toward differences and similarities in expression, further enhancing the meaning.

Where Can You Find These Techniques Now?

You can find parallelism in literature in addition to everyday speech. Let's have a look at some of the examples.

Parallelism in the Bible

Parallelism is found in the Bible, specifically in psalm proverbs and verses. One use of this literary device in Biblical poetry and phrasing is to develop synonymous lines where a poignant idea is presented. It is then repeated after being rephrased with parallelism. This is done to emphasise or reinforce meaning. Let's have a look at some of the examples from the Bible.

- *"The earth is the Lord's and everything in it / the world, and all who live in it "*- Ps. 24

- *"For the Lord knows the way of the righteous / But the way of the ungodly shall perish"*- Ps, 1:6

- *"As the deer pants for the water brooks / So pants my soul for You, O God "*-Ps. 42:1

- *"Hatred stirs up strife / But love covers all sins"* - Prov. 10:12

- "In *the way of righteousness is life / And in its pathway, there is no death*" -Prov. 12:28

- "*I am the rose of Sharon / And the lily of the valleys* "- Song 2:1

Popular examples of parallelism

- "*But the sad truth is that the truth is sad and that what you want does not matter*". - Lemony Snicket

- "*Follow love, and it will flee; flee love, and it will follow.*" - Proverb

- "*Be who you are and say what you feel because those who mind don't matter, and those who matter don't mind.*" - Bernard M. Baruch

- "*Then practice losing farther, losing faster: places, and names, and where it was you meant to travel. None of these will bring disaster*". - Elizabeth Bishop

- "*You deserve to need me, not to have me*". - Augusten Burroughs

- "*Not everything that is faced can be changed, but nothing can be changed until it is faced*". - James Baldwin

- *"And that government of the people, by the people, for the people shall not perish from the earth".* - Abraham Lincoln

- *"Clap along if you feel like a room without a roof / Clap along if you feel like happiness is the truth"* - Lyrics by Pharrell Williams

Examples of parallelism in rhetoric

Parallelism in rhetoric is designed to motivate, persuade, or evoke emotional responses in the audience and is used in various speeches. The proper balance between phrases or clauses helps make complex thoughts much easier to process while also holding the listener's or reader's attention. Parallelism has a different meaning, relying on context. However, it also involves balancing the structure or weight of phrases or ideas. In rhetoric, it's all about balancing two or more arguments or opinions on the same level. Some of the examples of parallelism in rhetoric are:

- *"We've seen the unfurling of flags, the lighting of candles, the giving of blood, the saying of prayers."* - George W. Bush.

- *My fellow citizens: I stand here today humbled by the task before us, grateful for the trust you have bestowed, mindful of the sacrifices borne by our ancestors."* - Barack Obama

- *"One small step for man, one giant leap for mankind."* - Neil Armstrong

- *"For the end of theoretical science is truth, but the end of a practical science is performance."* - Aristotle

- *"Today's students can put dope in their veins or hope in their brains. If they can conceive it and believe it, they can achieve it. They must know it is not their aptitude but their attitude that will determine their altitude."* -Jesse Jackson

- *"I have a dream that my four little children will one day live in a nation where they will not be judged by the colour of their skin but by the content of their character. I have a dream today."* - Martin Luther King, Jr.

Example of parallelism in literature

Parallelism is an excellent literary device when used appropriately. Let's look at an example of parallelism and how it helps add significance to famous works of literature.

*"If you can't appreciate what you have got,
you'd better get what you can appreciate."*

This line is from George Bernard Shaw's famous play Pygmalion. Shaw uses parallelism to contrast ideas by inverting the phrase wordings whilst maintaining grammatical structure. Because of parallelism, this line demonstrates the relationship between what someone has and what they can appreciate. Professor Higgins's speaker of the line calls Eliza's attention to the choice she's struggling with – either she understands what she has in him as a partner or chooses someone else. The use of parallelism underscores the choice between the contrasting ideas in the line by Shaw in its expression.

How to Introduce It Into Everyday Language?

As an effective literary device, parallelism creates a harmonious rhythm and flow of phrases and words. It's practical because it captures the reader's attention and improves the structure to make it more meaningful. Parallelism is also an excellent way for the writers to develop relationships between two or more ideas or things through contrast or comparison. Use parallelism sparingly in everyday language as excessive repetition of the grammatical elements might fatigue or distract the audience.

For instance, a well-known parallelism proverb is – *"Give a man a fish, and he eats for a day. Teach a man to fish, and he eats for a lifetime."* It's effective as the repetition of the sentence structure focuses on the perceived meaning of the proverb. But if the same proverb had to continue the repetitive form, it would lose its effectiveness. For instance - *"Give a man a fish, and he eats for a day. Teach a man to fish, and he eats for a lifetime. Teach a man to sell fish, and he eats meat. Give a man a chain of restaurants, and he eats anything he wants."*

The continuous parallelism undermines the actual meaning of the proverb. Some more examples of parallelism in everyday language:

- *Stupid is as stupid does.*

- *You get what you get.*

- *Luck is the idol of the idle.*

- *Where there's smoke, there is fire.*

- *No pain and no gain.*

Chapter 11:

It's Not the Importance of Antithesis, It's How You Use It

The English language is rich with various literary devices that can easily lift your writing or speaking and one such tool is antithesis. Antithesis means opposite or a contrast; for instance, when someone or something is the opposite of the other person or thing. As an effective rhetorical device, antithesis pairs opposite ideas in parallel grammatical structure. For example, consider the famous line from William Shakespeare's Hamlet – "*Give every man thy ear, but few thy voice.*" This is an excellent example of antithesis as it ends to pairs two completely contrasting ideas – speaking and listening – in the same parallel structure.

Why Use Antithesis?

Antithesis means "opposite." It is generally the exact opposite of a concept, statement, or idea. In literary analysis, an antithesis is a pair of images or messages that reverses the other. The couple is established with the same grammatical structures to showcase a higher degree of contrast. It is used to emphasise an idea, concept, or conclusion. The effect of antithesis can be pretty powerful. Using it accurately can distinguish between those opposing views simply by positioning them side-by-side in the same structure. When you use it in an argument, how all these ideas are placed can make it obvious which is better.

In addition, antithesis is used to create rhythm, as antithesis often uses parallelism. In simple terms, it sets up a repetitive structure that helps in making the writing sound musical. Consider the famous opening of Charles Dickens's A Tale Of Two Cities – *"It was the best of times, it was the worst of times."*

What's the Effect of Doing This and How Does It Help Convince People?

Antithesis might be a little tricky to notice at first. To start with, notice how each of the sentences is separated into two different parts. The parts are generally separated either by using a semicolon, a dash or the word "but." Keep in mind that antithesis always comes with a multi-part structure. The parts may not be that obvious; however, they'll be there all the time. As contrast is highlighted side-by-side with the same design, the speaker can impact the audience significantly and be more memorable.

- *"The world will little note, nor long remember what we say here, but it can never forget what they did here."* – Abraham Lincoln.

- *"I have a dream that my four little children will one day live in a nation where they will not be judged by the colour of their skin but by the content of their character."* – Martin Luther King Jr.

In these examples, notice how the second part of each consists of a term that inverts or reverses the terms of the first part – "*remember vs forge*t" or "*colour of skin vs content of character.*" This is another common theme of antithesis. Notice that antithesis always contains a parallel idea and structure to support the opposition. Both parts are not merely simple contradictory statements; they work as a matched pair of several grammatical concepts or designs but are opposites. For instance in, *"one small step for a man, one giant leap for mankind"* the word "*one*" is followed by an adjective, noun, and then "*for.*" Doing this accentuates the opposites simply by setting them up against a backdrop of sameness. Simply put, two completely different ideas get expressed with very similar grammatical structures. So, in an antithesis, you have:

- Two or more portions
- Inverted or reversed ideas
- Parallel grammatical structure

Importance of antithesis

Antithesis is a complex nature of juxtaposition. The effects are similar – by opposing one thing against another, a speaker or writer can emphasise the primary attributes of what they're speaking about. For example, in the quote, *"one small step for a man, one giant leap for mankind"* by Neil Armstrong, the extreme significance of the very first step on the moon is made solid and vivid by opposing it with the ordinariness and smallness of the motion of stepping. Use antithesis for expressing curious paradoxes or contradictions. Neil Armstrong invited the listeners to become confused but highly engaged over an ordinary, tiny step – not dissimilar from the millions of steps that we take every day – representing the massive technological accomplishment of landing on the moon. You can also use antithesis to showcase how two opposite things might be similar.

Related terms – Juxtaposition

Juxtaposition is a device that encompasses any kind of deliberate usage of contradiction or contrast by a writer. So as with antithesis, it can include:

- Any one of several expressions, like
  a. Mountain and sea
  b. Heaven and hell
  c. In sickness and in health

- The movie "The Godfather" is a series of murders intercut with various baptism shots, juxtaposing death and birth.

Antithesis does something very similar; however, it does so in a complicated way by utilising complete sentences.

Who Uses It Now?

There are various examples of antithesis in literature, pop culture, and advertising.

Example of antithesis in literature

Example #1

"Forgive us this day our trespasses as we forgive those trespass against us." – The Lord's Prayer.

In this example, antithesis is working over-
time. Firstly, it showcases the parallel connection
between committing an evil act and being the victim of one. We know that these are the exact opposites, and this knowledge is a part of antithesis.
However, at the same time, they are the same act
from different perspectives in the end. Thus, antithesis is an expression of this golden rule. Secondly, the antithesis also displays a parallel between the speaker and the other person (God).
The line above is a request for divine mercy, and
at the same time, is a gentle reminder that human beings need to be merciful as well.

Example #2

*"All the joy the world consists of has come
through wanting happiness for other people. All
the misery the world consists of has come
through wanting pleasure for oneself."* – The
Way of the Bodhisattva, Shantideva

Here, the antithesis comes with a massive, in-
tense parallel structure. The majority of the
words in the sentences are the same as that of the
other sentence. Such a similar structure helps to
make the antithesis even more striking, as the
terms that differ become more visible. Another
feature of this antithesis is that it makes "happiness" and "pleasure" seem like opposites. But we

171

know that both are more or less synonymous. This quote makes happiness seem holy and noble, where pleasure is displayed as worthless and selfish.

Example of antithesis in pop culture

Most of us aren't aware that you can also find antithesis in pop culture.

Example #1

"What men must know, a boy must learn." – The Lookouts

Here is an excellent example of how parallel structure can turn into antithesis quickly. The antithesis also helps to express the basic narrative of The Lookouts, which is mainly about kids learning to become adults.

Example #2

"Shut your mouth, and open your eyes." – the band A.F.I.

Here, the antithesis is a juxtaposition of two variable actions – opening and shutting. Yet, they are part of the same behaviour – the behaviour of someone wishing to understand the world instead of being the centre of attention. It's a rehash of the old saying – *"Those who speak the most have got the least to say."*

Example of antithesis in advertising and speech

For years, speakers have used figures of speech for persuasion. Some examples;

- *"Folks who have no vices have very few virtues".* – Abraham Lincoln

- *"Patience is bitter, but it has a sweet fruit".* – Aristotle

- *"Everybody doesn't like something, but nobody doesn't like Sara Lee."* – Advertising slogan of Sara Lee

- *"Integrity without knowledge is weak and useless, and knowledge without integrity is dangerous and dreadful".* – Samuel Johnson

How to Introduce It Into Everyday Language?

As antithesis is a complex device in rhetoric and is tied to the meaning of particular sentences, it's always better to use it with a plan, specifically in technical writing or research papers. Instead, just allow the antithesis to appear where it would naturally. As antithesis emphasises a particular conclusion or point, you can use it in everything, from prose and poetry to advertising and speech.

173

However, if you force antithesis into your writing or speaking, you may risk distorting what you want to say or at least end up making it unclear. Therefore, instead of trying to practice antithesis directly, use parallel structure. You'll eventually create practical antithesis naturally, however, only when your meaning requires it.

The parallel structure uses the same types of words and grammatical structure in two portions of a sentence. For instance,

- As you play with guns, you're inviting trouble.

Structure – "you," followed by verb, preposition, and then a noun

- Bring me a platter and play me a piece of music.

Structure – verb, followed by "me," "a," and noun

- He wrote the book, taught the class, and graded his students.

Structure – verb, followed by "the," and then noun

These examples are not antithesis but are sentences that come with parallel structures. Let's have a look at some examples that have parallel structures as well as antithesis.

- *I love the sinner but hate the sin.*

    Structure – imperative verb followed by "the" and then a noun

- *She was brave in words but a coward in her deeds.*

    Structure – adjective followed by "in" and then a plural noun

Antithesis is a superb way of adding contrast to your writing and speaking. To use antithesis to best effect, follow these tips.

- **Paying attention to contrast:** Think of all those places in your writing that might benefit from comparing two contrasting themes or ideas. For example, in creative fictional writing, is there a character who's dealing with their emotions? Is there are a scene that includes negative attributes? The two concepts don't need to be the exact opposite; however, they must be distinct and different enough to work, such as frustration and excitement.

- **Reading it aloud:** As you work on your parallel structure, you want the rhythm of each of the pieces to feel as similar as possible. If you get stuck, read the line aloud to determine where the syllables may not fit. Keep in mind that the parallel structure of antithesis doesn't need to be exact; however, the closer they are in the system, the more rhythmic it should sound.

- **Use it sparingly:** As with all convincing rhetorical devices, antithesis is best when used sparingly. If you overuse it, you might risk your writing or speech sounding forced or tired. So, use it only when necessary.

Conclusion

Thank you for reading the entirety of *Winning them Over: Discover the Secret of Language That Changes Minds*;   I hope it was informative and that I could provide you with the foundation you need to achieve your goals, whatever they may be.

Rhetoric is the principle of communication and is helpful for those who want to inform or persuade. It includes several figures of speech discussed in this book, and I hope you go on to use them now you understand how they work.

Alliteration is a powerful device for persuading others. It uses a sequence of words where the starting or initial letters are the same. You can either place the terms next to each other space them out. Such a rhetorical device acts just like a hammer that helps in beating the point. Using alliteration in threes is regarded as the most effective usage. The overall effect of alliteration is poetic and makes everything seem comfortable and pleasant to the audience's ears.

Next comes the use of rhyme. Use all those words that rhyme with each other – repeating the

177

same sound across several words. Use a poetic meter or only words that end with the same sound scattered throughout your sentences. The word endings that rhyme can either be exact tonal matches or just similar. You could also choose internal rhyme, where the sounds and letters get repeated across a sentence. The more you use the words like a poem, the less natural it will sound. To achieve subtle communication, try to scatter all the rhyming words randomly throughout your speech.

At the heart of persuasive speaking is that the audience understands everything you're communicating. As the audience comes to know what you say, it results in acceptance. In this sense, analogies are tough to beat. The majority of the persuasive power of analogies comes from the listeners or audience understanding on their own. Using analogy in your speech makes the communication more persuasive. It shows how two things are similar; but in a more complex way.

Metaphor is another tool of persuasion that works by combining two disparate concepts or ideas. First, it is a potent tool of communication that helps others take your concepts or ideas into consideration in brand-new ways. Use them right at the start of your sentence. Using them at the end or in the middle will give them zero impact. Secondly, metaphor needs to associate with the context of your statement or argument. If used correctly, it can make the most complex subjects more accessible for the audience to understand.

Choose similes for a better projection of your message. A simile is the figure of speech that compares two unlikely things with the use of two words – "as" or "like." You can find simile in everyday communication, and you can use it to spark interest in the mind of the audience or reader. For example, comparing two different things with "like" or "as" helps make the message clearer in the audience's mind. As a result, they picture the situation and understand its true meaning.

Amplification of a statement can help you project your message more effectively in the audience's direction. It's about expanding and enriching a description to create more importance. For example, if you say, "*The tree fell,*" it doesn't project much impact. But if you say, "*The large tree right around the corner of the street, with big trunks and lots of vines fell because of the twister,*" it creates more impact in the minds of the audience. Your aim should be to provide as much detail as possible for better persuasion.

If you want to add emphasis on a statement or subject, choose hyperbole. Hyperbole involves exaggeration from you as the speaker for the sake of emphasis. They should be exaggerations to emphasise a point instead of being taken literally. Saying, "*My bag weighs a ton*" does not mean that the bag weighs a ton. It adds emphasis to the weight of the bag. The bag carrier wants to communicate with the use of hyperbole that they're carrying a heavy load.

Making an object or idea come to life can help you communicate better. The same is done with personification. When you present an object or a thought with human-like characteristics, it makes your content more interactive. It makes descriptions more unique, so the audience can connect to what you say, or the readers can relate to what you write.

Another influential figure of speech that can help to persuade others is parallelism. With this, you need to provide two or more elements of vocabulary or sentences with the same grammatical structure. This might also involve the repetition of the exact words. But, again, make sure you use the same grammatical elements; otherwise, it's not parallelism.

Creating opposition between two different things for the sake of establishing a critical message is termed antithesis; you need to bring out the contrast in your thoughts or ideas by using noticeable differences in clauses, sentences, or words.

I hope this book provided you with the necessary foundation and tools to persuade your audience or readers, the techniques that we've discussed here can be applied both to your professional and personal life.

Finally, if you found this book valuable, a review on Amazon is always very much appreciated! Thank you

Resources

(n.d.-a). Smartblogger. Retrieved July 29, 2021, from https://smartblogger.com/alliteration-examples/

. (n.d.-b). Smartblogger. Retrieved July 29, 2021, from https://smartblogger.com/metaphor-examples/

Alliteration. (n.d.). Literary Terms. Retrieved July 29, 2021, from https://literaryterms.net/alliteration/

Amplification. (n.d.). Literary Terms. Retrieved July 29, 2021, from https://literaryterms.net/amplification/

Amplification - Examples and Definition of Amplification. (n.d.). Literary Devices. Retrieved July 29, 2021, from https://literarydevices.net/amplification/

Analogy. (n.d.). Changing. Retrieved July 29, 2021, from http://changingminds.org/techniques/language/figures_speech/analogy.htm

Analogy Examples With Simple Explanations. (n.d.). Yourdictionary. Retrieved July 29, 2021, from https://examples.yourdictionary.com/analogy-ex.html

Attention Required! | Cloudflare. (n.d.-a). Masterclass. Retrieved July 29, 2021, from https://www.masterclass.com/articles/writing-101-what-is-rhetoric-learn-about-rhetorical-devices-in-writing-and-3-modes-of-persuasion-in-rhetoric#what-is-a-rhetorical-device

Attention Required! | Cloudflare. (n.d.-b). Masterclass. Retrieved July 29, 2021, from https://www.masterclass.com/articles/what-is-analogy#quiz-0

Attention Required! | Cloudflare. (n.d.-c). Masterclass. Retrieved July 29, 2021, from https://www.masterclass.com/articles/what-is-simile#quiz-0

Attention Required! | Cloudflare. (n.d.-d). Masterclass. Retrieved July 29, 2021, from https://www.masterclass.com/articles/what-is-simile#what-is-the-difference-between-simile-and-metaphor

Attention Required! | Cloudflare. (n.d.-e). Myassignmenthelp. Retrieved July 29, 2021, from https://myassignmenthelp.com/blog/personification-in-persuasive-writing/

Attention Required! | Cloudflare. (n.d.-f). Masterclass. Retrieved July 29, 2021, from https://www.masterclass.com/articles/how-to-use-antithesis-in-your-writing#quiz-0

Beqiri, G. (2018, June 12). *Rhetoric: How to Inform, Persuade, or Motivate your Audience.* Virtual Speech. https://virtualspeech.com/blog/rhetoric-inform-persuade-motivate-your-audience

Difference Between Simile and Metaphor (with Examples and Comprison Chart). (n.d.). Key Differences. Retrieved July 29, 2021, from https://keydifferences.com/difference-between-simile-and-metaphor.html

Effective Communication: the Power of Metaphor. (n.d.). Communispond. Retrieved July 29, 2021, from https://communispond.com/insights/blog/415/effective-communication-the-power-of-metaphor/

Examples of Amplification in Literature. (n.d.). Yourdictionary. Retrieved July 29, 2021, from https://examples.yourdictionary.com/examples-of-amplification-in-literature.html

Examples of Antithesis Across Mediums. (n.d.). Yourdictionary. Retrieved July 29, 2021, from https://examples.yourdictionary.com/examples-of-antithesis.html

Examples of Hyperbole: What It Is and How to Use It. (n.d.). Yourdictionary. Retrieved July 29, 2021, from https://examples.yourdictionary.com/examples-of-hyperboles.html

Examples of Parallelism in Literature and Rhetoric. (n.d.). Yourdictionary. Retrieved July 29, 2021, from https://examples.yourdictionary.com/examples-of-parallelism.html

Examples of Rhetoric: Tools to Persuade and Motivate. (n.d.). Your Dictionary. Retrieved July 29, 2021, from https://examples.yourdictionary.com/examples-of-rhetoric.html

How to Identify Metaphors in a Poem. (n.d.). Pen and the Pad. Retrieved July 29, 2021, from https://penandthepad.com/identify-metaphors-poem-5124.html

How To Use Similes, Analogies and Metaphors | Writing Speeches. (n.d.). Word Nerds. Retrieved July 29, 2021, from https://www.word-nerds.com.au/writing-speeches-using-similes-metaphors-and-analogies/

Hyperbole - Examples and Definition of Hyperbole as Literary Device. (n.d.). Literary Devices. Retrieved July 29, 2021, from https://literarydevices.net/hyperbole/

Hyperbole: Public Speaking/Speech Communication. (n.d.). Lumen. Retrieved July 29, 2021, from https://lumen.instructure.com/courses/218897/pages/linkedtext54256?module_item_id=5007121

Literary Techniques: Simile | Matrix Literary Techniques. (n.d.). Matrix Education. Retrieved July 29, 2021, from https://www.matrix.edu.au/literary-techniques-simile/

Metaphor Examples: Understanding Meaning and Purpose. (n.d.). Yourdictionary. Retrieved July 29, 2021, from https://examples.yourdictionary.com/metaphor-examples.html

Metaphors - Winning Your Audience's Heart - Learn - Persuading Others - Harvard Manage-Mentor. (n.d.). Byui. Retrieved July 29, 2021, from https://www2.byui.edu/HMM10/persuading_others/metaphors.html

Parallelism - Examples and Definition of Parallelism. (n.d.). Literary Devices. Retrieved July 29, 2021, from https://literarydevices.net/parallelism/

Personification: Public Speaking/Speech Communication. (n.d.). Lumen. Retrieved July 29, 2021, from https://lumen.instructure.com/courses/218897/pages/linkedtext54258?module_item_id=5007123

The Persuasive Power of Analogy. (2021, May 24). Copyblogger. https://copyblogger.com/persuasive-analogies/

Post author: admin. (n.d.). Aas. Retrieved July 29, 2021, from https://www.allassignmentservices.com/blog/importance-of-personification-in-persuasive-writing/

The Power and Influence of Analogies. (n.d.). Stu Schlackman. Retrieved July 29, 2021, from https://stuschlackman.com/communications-skills/the-power-and-influence-of-analogies/

The Rhetorical Strategy of Amplification in an Argument. (n.d.). ThoughtCo. Retrieved July 29, 2021, from https://www.thoughtco.com/what-is-amplification-rhetoric-1689086

The Rhyme-as-Reason Effect: Why Rhyming Makes Your Message More Persuasive. (n.d.). Effectiviology. Retrieved July 29, 2021, from https://effectiviology.com/rhyme-as-reason/

The role of metaphor in communication and thought. (n.d.). Wiley Online Library. Retrieved July 29, 2021, from https://onlinelibrary.wiley.com/doi/abs/10.1111/lnc3.12327

Rule of Three in Speech Writing. (2018, January 9). Dave Linehan. https://davelinehan.com/rule-of-three-speechwriting/

Save Time, Persuade with Rhyme! (2014, August 6). Neuromarketing. https://www.neurosciencemarketing.com/blog/articles/rhyme.htm

Types of persuasive language techniques : Alliteration, simile, metaphor. . .. (2020, February 17). AllAssignmentHelp.Com - Best Academic Helper US and Australia. https://www.allassignmenthelp.com/blog/persuasive-language-techniques/

Use Metaphors to Persuade: Take a page from Seth Godin. (n.d.). Sticky Branding. Retrieved July 29, 2021, from https://stickybranding.com/use-metaphors-to-persuade-take-a-page-from-seth-godin/?sfw=pass1626117289

Using Other Supporting Materials | Boundless Communications. (n.d.). Lumenlearning. Retrieved July 29, 2021, from https://courses.lumenlearning.com/boundless-communications/chapter/using-other-supporting-materials/

What is Alliteration — Definitions, Examples in Literature & Film. (2021, July 4). StudioBinder.

https://www.studiobinder.com/blog/what-is-allit-eration-definition/

What Is Personification In Persuasive Writing? (n.d.). Peatix. Retrieved July 29, 2021, from https://peatix.com/group/7248194

Why is Rhetoric Required? | Department of Rhetoric | College of Liberal Arts & Sciences | The University of Iowa. (n.d.). Uiowa. Retrieved July 29, 2021, from https://clas.uiowa.edu/rhetoric/about/why-is-rhetoric-required

Why rhyming phrases are more persuasive. (2015, December 16). Gizmodo. https://gizmodo.-com/why-rhyming-phrases-are-more-persuasive-1524861998

Made in United States
North Haven, CT
29 June 2023

38363128R00104